Also from Telling Our Stories Press

ROLL: A Collection of Personal Narratives
SURVIVE: A Collection of Short Memoirs
TURNS: A Collection of Memoir Chapbooks
SO LONG: Short Memoirs of Loss and Remembrance
THE BRIDGE: A Companion Journal for Unearthing
Personal Narratives and Memoir
RESURRECTING PROUST: Unearthing Personal
Narratives through Journaling
MY CIA: A Memoir

Praise for
IMPACT

"Who says memoirs have to be long? In fact, who says they even have to be prose? IMPACT: An Anthology of Short Memoirs edited by CoCo Harris, provides a convincing and highly entertaining answer to those questions—which is a resounding, They don't. They just need to be good. And you'll find plenty of good in IMPACT."
—Richard Goodman, author of *French Dirt: The Story of a Garden in the South of France, The Soul of Creative Writing, A New York Memoir* and *The Bicycle Diaries: One New Yorker's Journey Through 9-11*

"As an inspired laboratory for the reinvention of the memoir genre, IMPACT is a superb must-read, rich in snapshot takes on the human heart; insights unsettling, even disturbing but always moving."
—Alan Kaufman, author of the memoirs *Drunken Angel and Jew Boy*

"Profoundly sensitive and intelligent, Impact offers the reader a wide range of aesthetic and personal perspectives. Stephen King has made the comment that everyone has a story and that most of them are boring. CoCo Harris has culled through stories and found the ones that matter, the ones that move and excite, the ones that achieve art through the evocation of the universal through the personal."
—Mark Spencer, author of *A Haunted Love Story, The Masked Demon,* and *The Weary Motel*

"A poet once said, "Out of our sadness have we made the world so beautiful." But as the poems and stories of IMPACT make abundantly clear, the "beautiful" also can be made out of joy and anger, fear and delight and adventure."
—Alan Steinberg, author of *Cry of the Leopard, Fathering,* and *The Road to Corinth*

"From "First Trip Abroad" and the "isosceles hats" of Spain, thru the "airplane that came out of the sky" in "Who am I?" this is an aha ride into serrated memories. Absolutely top-notch! These poems and stories never fail to delight and surprise. IMPACT: An Anthology of Short Memoirs is sharp-witted and concise."
—Sheryl L. Nelms, Fiction/Nonfiction Editor NLAPW magazine, *The Pen Woman*

"Discoveries of the examined life are never without impact, either on the self and those connected, or on future generations, readers of this expertly-edited anthology have a window to a wide range of interesting lives. Here are stories as fascinating, heart-wrenching and uplifting as experience itself, stories bearing a common stamp of humanity's striving toward understanding. The compiled poems and short memoir are written with such articulate insight that we not only want to know these people, we are also inspired to examine our own lives with as much compassion and openness to the vagaries of destiny.

"Meet the granddaughter of a Russian survivor whose biography is punctuated by parallels to Anna Karina; the boy who is told in a myriad of dictates; "this is how you" not become a sissy; and the grandmother who finds balm for her loss in the life of her new grandchild. Ponder decisions as monumental as how best to provide for the gestating child, as telling as how next to decorate the fireplace mantle. Join these engaging individuals "connecting up the parts" and "making friends with all of it.""
—Maureen Tolman Flannery, author of *Tunnel into Morning*,
Destiny Whispers to the Beloved, and *Ancestors in the Landscape*

"…By freeze-framing different memories/moments, we are led to examine and perhaps draw insight. For writers of memoir, looking back on an entire life is sometimes overwhelming like attempting a marathon, but by breaking it down and taking it one step at a time, we can find joy in the journey. The book's strength is that one memory or entry in the anthology usually led me down a path of my own memories…."
—Jane Hertenstein, author of *Home is Where We Live: Life at a Shelter Through a Young Girl's Eyes, Orphan Girl: The Memoir of a Chicago Bag Lady* (with Marie James), and *Beyond Paradise*

"Upon reading IMPACT, I was blown away by the imaginative prose, insightful reflections, and searing tales of love, loss, vulnerability, and desire. From Eleanor Vincent's touching story of new life and lingering death, Weitzman's familiar yet deeply emotional reflections on elder care and the helplessness felt by the parent and adult child, Oleskewicz's biting commentary on the public's inability to understand the strength and humanity in disability to Reid-Pharr's brilliant account of family dynamics which re-categorize dysfunction into pockets of strange normalcy; there are very few selections in this volume that do not stay with the reader long after the pages are turned. Personal favorites are Walters re-imagining of Jamaica Kincaid's much anthologized "Girl" using the voice of a father and his son, and Poku's endearing treatment of the war between a man's God and his devil. Bravo to the authors and to CoCo Harris for compiling such an intriguing text.
—Kalenda Eaton, author of *Womanism, Literature, and the Transformation of the Black Community*, 1965-1980

"Impact features prose and poetic vignettes narrating single, substantial moments that often change the directions of individual lives. Often intensely personal, these narrative moments provide glimpses into the very soul of a stranger and, by extension, into the reader's own heart and life. A deeply thoughtful and satisfying collection!"
—Lori Watkins Fulton, author of *William Faulkner, Gavin Stevens, and the Cavalier Tradition*

IMPACT

IMPACT

An Anthology of
Short Memoirs

CoCo Harris

TELLING OUR STORIES PRESS

Telling the Telling Our Stories of Our Lives Press

Showcasing the Art of Literary Personal Narratives

Published by Telling Our Stories Press

The independent literary imprint with a focus on
the art of short memoir and personal narratives.

Requests for information should be forwarded to:
Telling Our Stories Press
www.TellingOurStoriesPress.com

Cover Photograph: "Water and Stones"
by Janos and Maria Mathiesen
Cover Design: Michael Milliken & CoCo Harris
Book Layout: Renee Nixon and Chris Schramm

"The Only Boy in Ballet Class" was previously published in *Stoneboat* and
in *My Mother and the Ceiling Dancers* by Zack Rogow (Kattywompus Press).
"First Trip Abroad" was previously published in *My Mother and
the Ceiling Dancers* by Zack Rogow (Kattywompus Press).
An earlier version of "And Never Said Hello" was previously published in
PaniK: Candid Stories of Life Altering Experience Surrounding Pregnancy
as "Grass from the Grave."

UltraShort Memoir™ is a trademark of Telling Our Stories Press

Library of Congress Control Number: 2011940100
Printed in the United States of America

ISBN-13: 978-0982922866

ISBN-10: 0982922868

for

Marcus

and
as always

The O-Girls

Acknowledgements

A special thanks to all those on the Telling Our Stories Press Advisory Council; and to all the Galley Reviewers who took the time to graciously provide critical comments, hearty suggestions, and necessary edits. These wonderful folks include Mom, George Shields, Gregg Weatherby, Zack Rogow, Nancy Prothro Arbuthnot, Tim Taylor, Clayton Scott, Amber West, Chris Donovan, Rebecca T. Dickinson, Carmen A. Fiore, and Lisa Dale Norton.

Deep appreciation to all those who shared the stories of their lives such that this volume, of our collective story, can exist.

CONTENTS

Ultrashort Introduction

CORNERS

Zack Rogow 4
First Trip Abroad
The Only Boy in Ballet Class
A Small Knowledge

Eleanor Vincent 9
Lucia's Birth

Sarah Brown Weitzman 18
Nothing For You
The Forgetting
Measuring Spoons
Under the Yellow Ceiling

Jacqueline Kolosov 23
Re-reading Anna Karenina

Mac Greene 34
A Life in 100 Words

Mariangela Mihai 35
Balcony

Kristin Laurel 40
The Burn Unit

Jasminne Mendez 43
I Miss You

DaMaris B. Hill 44
Glory Days

W. Clayton Scott 45
Colors of Hardware
Sounds of Human Comfort
Elements of Reconsideration

Alex Stein 50
Desperate Characters

Rikki Santer 57
   Mother to Son
   Overleaf
   Mourning Sickness
Casey Clabough 60
   Show & Tell
Kirby Wright 69
   Black Butterfly
Bradley Earle Hoge 70
   geometry of poetry
Janine Lehane 71
   Diorama
Diane Hoover Bechtler 74
   Armed
Deborah L. J. Mackinnon 75
   Cat Scratches
J.D. Blair 77
   Doc Su
Regina Murray Brault 78
   1947 Family Portrait
Debra Baker 79
   Losing Shawn, Losing Me
Deni Ann Gereighty 91
   Change of Life
   Moon
   Number 1 Grandchild
Lewis Gardner 94
   Memory
Sarah Glenn Fortson 96
   I Will Remember Now

ABOUT FACE

Exsulo Illustro 100
   Level 101:

Elayne Clift...101
   Writing My Mother's Life
Douglas G. Campbell...103
   I Don't Stand Up When They Play Dixie
Karen de Balbian Verster 104
   Answered Prayers
Dorothy Stone...110
   Two Looks Back
Nancy Skalla 114
   Sounds of a Woman's Growth
Nicole Zimmerman 115
   Shasta in Stanzas
Dave Morrison..116
   Namesake
Nancy Lubarsky 118
   What If, As Your Sister Claimed
Alan Cohen 119
   Here Comes Dad, 1947
Ahrend R. Torrey...120
   Boy
Nan Rush...122
   I Dress in Red
Barbara Tatro 131
   Mannequin
Carol J. Rhodes 132
   Big Shoes to Fill
Mamie Potter 133
   The Golf Course Grass
Terry Martin...134
   In the Space Provided Below, Tell Us About Yourself
   Ongoing Conversation
Summer DeNaples 137
   For Painter and Brides
Beth Lynn Clegg 138
   The Four-Poster

Susan Grier.. 139
   Goodbye
Beth Winegarner 141
   Half Empty
Tamara W 142
   That Old Life
Madeleine Beckman 143
   A Great Pass
Christine Donovan... 144
   Gathering Flowers in My Father's Garden
Raud Kennedy 152
   Making My Own Acquaintance
   Meeting my Past
Ann Mintz.. 154
   A Fate Worse than Death
Russ Allison Loar 155
   My Father Among the Chinese

CRUXES

Yu-Han Chao 158
   Why I Did Not Become a World-Famous Classical Violinist
Helen Ruggieri.. 164
   Haibun
Linda Mussillo.. 169
   Ordering
Cari Oleskewicz... 170
   Notes for My Therapist
Carmen Anthony Fiore.. 174
   Open Letter to My Dead Mother
Amber L. West 175
   Untitled
Catherine Lee 176
   East Coast

Robert F. Reid-Pharr 177
    The Cleaning Man's Son
W. K. Medlen 185
    God's Blood
    The Story of Fathers
Cherri Randall 189
    Daughter Rhymes with Laughter
Judith Serin 194
    Some Family Stories
Barbara Lewis 199
    Time Exposure
Shelly Clark Geiser 200
    Writing the Memoir
Rebecca T. Dickinson 202
    We Never Said Hello
Monica Macansantos 208
    James
Richard Ballon 210
    That Green Land of Light and Shadow
Paul Sohar 211
    The River
Gina Ferrara 210
    Money, Missippi (1966)
Martha Everhart Braniff 211
    Humming Birds at Midnight
Gregg Weatherby 212
    Approaching Home
    Mom's Chair
    Old House Winter
    Equinox
    Ashes
    Sweet Water
Noelle Sickels 222
    The Hedge

Alba Poku.. 223
  Father's Affair
Margaret Elysia Garcia.. 224
  Shalom Ma Ze
David Breeden 229
  Nineteen Fifty Eight
Gloria Jean Harris 231
  Who am I?
CoCo Harris.. 233
  I am

CONTRIBUTORS

ABOUT THE EDITOR

Between the words we speak
and the life we seek
there is always
so much space.

—Rick Smith, *"With Olivia on Mingus Mountain"*

ULTRASHORT INTRODUCTION

"Impact has traditionally only been a noun. In recent years, however, it has undergone a semantic shift that has allowed it to act like a verb."
—Usage Note impact, by Ed. Bryan Garner
Oxford American Writers Thesaurus

From the UltraShort memoir of roughly one hundred words, to the poems, images, lists and the varying short prose carried within these pages, they all speak to the impact that our experiences have on our lives, and ultimately our collective narrative.

We are, after all, our stories.

Can you hold these stories?

Can you sit with them as your own; these abbreviated passages, shouldering the metaphors by which we live?

CORNERS

First Trip Abroad

At twelve, I had just woken up from the dream
of playing second base in Yankee pinstripes.
Anything
that breached my indifference
I resented. But my mother had wanderlust
so we packed
way too many bags and hat boxes
and rode the Great Circle
across Atlantic skies.

I was the burlap coal sack
my mother and sister had to lug
from Rembrandt to Rembrandt.
At first only strange money
interested me: half-crowns and guineas,
they still had farthings.

Then the first shock—the ceiling
of Westminster Abbey
splaying its lavish fans,
like a procession of limestone peacocks.
Hmm, I thought.

And how could I ignore those
iron jungles overgrowing the Metro entrances,
Notre Dame's stained-glass roulettes,
and a busty Victory
flying around the Louvre.

Venice floated into my dreams
even before I left it,
a blend of city, flotilla,
and wild party!
That Italian *gioia di vivere*
we tasted at every countless-course lunch
and in Michelangelo's

Goliath-sized David
naked in public. I loved how he defied
Friar Savonarola.

Spain, though. Spain
was still a prisoner of the 1930s,
guarded by *Guardia Civil* vultures
with their isosceles hats
of patent leather.
The driver hated us Yankees for Franco
till the hill above Toledo.
Then the driver pointed
to the towers of the Alcazar and confessed
he'd been cornered there,
battling for his life and the Republic,
and my mother told him,
My friends, my friends, too.
He gave us sugar
to offer the giant gums of horses.

History gleamed
like a sword
with a mother-of-pearl hilt.
Now the map was alive
and I was in it.

The Only Boy in Ballet Class

I know what you're thinking
but it's not about that.

It's about galaxies
of Austrian crystal dimming
as I shifted in my scratchy velvet seat.
The curtain was hiked up
and suddenly the pancaked dancers,
the costumes, and cut-out castles
beamed more real than daylight.

"Look how the cavalier partners her," my mother nudged
during the pas de deux.
The male launched the prima ballerina, letting her
fly. "Look how masculine he is,"
my mother admired.

I knew she was placing in my hands a message
about sex, about how to love a woman.

But when does the cavalier get to shine? I wondered.

Only when he soloed, it turned out. Then he
                                        leaped into the music.
                    Suspended.
Stretching time.

And my mother's message about the pas de deux
didn't mention where
a woman's desire was hiding,
like a lost continent.

So I began my life as a lover
with an obstructed view. Then

I dated a divorcée
who didn't believe
a woman's pleasure

just tags along after.
I started to carry the guilt
of all men for that deliberate ignorance,
while she taught me to play her cavalier.

I learned that dance well,
but still I had to find the man
behind the ballerina,
the one who only leaped
when the stage was empty.

A Small Knowledge

I stole a bag of soldiers
when I was nine.
The little men, monochromatic, gray
plastic, invulnerable
to scrapes or jabs, had palms
already smoothed into cylinders
to grab weapons. My father
had died six years before. My mother
had secretly gone back to her first husband,
now remarried and with a son
close in age to me.

A phone call exposed the transgression.
I overheard and knew what had to follow:
"We've shopped there since you were born,
we've got a charge account at that store."
I could feel the disappointment
in my mother's voice.
"You could've bought whatever
you wanted. Why did have to you steal?"

I didn't know. I returned the booty
and apologized to the owner,
the sweetest woman.
I only knew
when I took
what didn't belong to me,
the blood shook
in all my veins.

Eleanor Vincent

Lucia's Birth

Meghan's water broke at eight o'clock on a Friday night. The Kaiser obstetrician insisted that she come to the hospital although there were no other signs of labor. She and her husband Todd lived only a few miles away, but the doctor was eager to have her admitted to the hospital for fear of infection.

"Nothing's happening, Mom," Meghan told me over the phone. "Stay home. Get some sleep."

I tossed and turned, restless and impatient to be with my daughter. Yet when the sun seeped through the blinds the next morning, I rose and started doing chores – feeding the cat, watering plants, even dusting. After my third cup of green tea I realized I was stalling. Was I hoping to create order in my world as I faced the unknowns of Meghan's labor? Giving Meghan and Todd time to bond before the birth? Or just plain scared?

Any parent who has lost a child is forever terrified of losing another. Eighteen years before this birth, my older daughter died: she had gone into an irreversible coma following a fall from a horse. Just nineteen, Maya was suddenly gone.

So the morning after Meghan went to the hospital I realized it would take every ounce of my strength to face a hospital room again, let alone the peril of a birth. When I finally arrived at the Kaiser hospital in San Francisco at 11 o'clock that morning my jeans were crisp and my shirt pressed, but my mind was a blur, as if the car had driven itself from Oakland across the Bay Bridge and magically deposited me in the hospital's parking garage.

Meghan greeted me with a hug and seemed jaunty for a woman who'd been counting the hours waiting for labor to begin. That afternoon passed like a family picnic, people in and out of the room, Meghan sitting on a huge sports ball even rounder than the arc of her belly. Every half hour Meghan paced the halls leaning on Todd's arm in hopes of starting contractions.

The nurse was patient and didn't immediately push Pitocin, the drug that induces labor, even though the obstetrician had. But as the afternoon wore on, Meghan grew impatient when there was no progress and agreed to have her labor chemically induced. Two hours after they started the hormone drip, contractions began in earnest, and the party atmosphere evaporated. As Meghan's pain spiked suddenly, I saw fear in Todd's eyes mirroring my

9

own. The nurse encouraged Meghan to labor in different positions – for now she was standing rocking from side to side next to her hospital bed.

"Uhhhhhnnnnnnnn," Meghan sang. "Ohhhhhhhh." I held her under her armpits, her arms resting on my shoulders, the globe of her belly pressed against me. My knees buckled under her doubleness, the coming baby. I ran after her pain, seconds behind, echoing each lament with a chant. "Uh huh, that's good, honey. Now breathe. OK. You're doing great."

When she was a toddler, I used to stand at the bottom of the staircase in our rented house as Meghan climbed the stairs, biting my lip to keep from bounding up and scooping her into my arms. Doubled over each stair tread, gripping the ratty orange carpet with dimpled fingers, she lifted one chubby leg, then the other, defying gravity. When she reached the halfway point, I'd step up a few stairs. She'd climb higher. I'd follow at a safe distance.

Now she climbed each rung of pain and I followed, keeping her company, wanting to be there to catch her.

Karen, the labor nurse, read the printout from the computer monitor and my granddaughter's heartbeats appeared – little black glyphs on a roll of paper spilling from the machine. I pushed Meghan's dark hair back from her forehead. As I coached Meghan through her next contraction Karen returned to the side of the bed. "Listen to your Mom, Meghan," she said. I've learned to give advice sparingly, so I grinned inwardly. "You're doing great," Karen crooned.

Meghan stared at Karen, pupils wide. The pains came on her and I felt her belly tighten and then the strange whale song erupted again, as if she were calling to her pod. I suddenly remembered how quickly intense pain isolates a laboring woman from everyone around her. Gently, Todd stroked Meghan's shoulders. I held her close.

"Good, sweetie. Now breathe." I swayed back and forth with her. Todd moved to her left side, rubbing her back.

Meghan hung her head and shook it from side to side. A thick rope of hair fell over her cheek as she swayed her belly and rump against the bed. I tried to keep time, swaying with her. Her moans carved the air.

"How does anyone do this?" she wailed. I tightened my grip. Todd caught my eye and we held on to each other across Meghan's back.

"This is so normal," Karen leaned in close, the crinkles around her eyes visible, her salt and pepper hair drawn back in a clip. She said each word slowly and precisely so Meghan would be sure to hear. "You're doing it just right."

The fetal monitor beeped, and the printer shuddered, spitting out more paper. Karen went to check. Contractions were lengthening.

When Meghan was an infant my mother suggested I read the novel *Kristin Lavransdatter* by Sigrid Undset, a story set in 12th century Norway. I loved the book partly because of its honest portrayal of motherhood and birth. Kristin's labor with her first child still makes me sweat each time I read it. She goes wild with fear, balking at each pain, writhing on her hands and knees in the straw. In desperation, the midwife brings in Kristin's husband and has her sit on his knee in hopes she will relax enough to deliver her child. In that era, birthing was women's work. Men were never invited so the midwife's decision was bold. In the end, Kristin gave birth to a healthy son, though it almost killed her.

Now, it was the 21st century and Meghan's labor was taking place in a well-equipped Kaiser Permanente hospital in San Francisco with a supportive husband and more drugs than a woman could ever want. Yet I felt I was still in the straw with Kristin. The veneer of modern medical options – the voodoo of technology – couldn't take away the terror in Meghan's eyes or the scalding fear in my heart. I had lost my other daughter to coma, watching her slip away in a hospital room just like this one.

So I held Meghan tight and rocked from one foot to the other like I did all those years ago when she woke in the night to nurse and I'd stand by her changing table swaying her in my arms singing "Hush little baby don't say a word, Papa's gonna buy you a mockingbird."

In the waiting room my ex-husband Ron sat with his fourth wife, coming in every hour or so for a few moments to stroke his daughter's forehead and offer encouragement. During one of these forays, when Meghan was singing her whale song, he looked at me and said, "How can you stand to see her in so much pain?"

I smiled and shrugged. I had no answer for him. How could I stand to see her climb the stairs, or swim across the length of the pool, or go to college? How had I endured my long career of letting go?

Meghan's first word was "moon," from all the black mornings we stood looking out the window after her two o'clock feeding. "Look Meghan. The moon, the moon," I would point out the window and chant to her. She said her first word, "Moon! Moon!" It emerged clear and sudden in the dark, the light of a full moon bathing her face.

The wordless language she spoke now filled me with just as much awe. I turned back to her. She was bathed in sweat and her despair reminded me of my own protesting wails the day she was born: "I can't do this. *I caaaan't*," I had wailed. My midwife Penny leaned over me, her white handprint on my red belly where she pushed to help the baby out, captured in one of the birth photos. When a contraction peaked and I screamed "No, no, NO," Penny whispered in my ear, "Say yes, Eleanor, say yes!" So I screamed "YES" with all my might and my daughter's head crowned. Meghan's victory over her pains seemed far from her now. But ultimately, it would come. Karen and I knew this. So we focused on the work at hand.

"Meghan told me she was born at home," Karen said during a moment when Meghan was resting. We looked at each other over my daughter's head. I nodded. Karen smiled. The lines around her eyes mapped a kind life. I liked how she planted her clogs on the linoleum and stood her ground. She looked like a ranch wife, stoic and practical, but not ungentle. It turned out she was from New Zealand and had been a midwife.

"You could be a doula," she said, "you're good at this."

"Thanks," I said, knowing that coming from Karen this was a high compliment.

After 6 hours of hard labor, my daughter was crestfallen and weary. She had hoped for few or no drugs, but her energy was flagging and all signs pointed toward more anesthesia.

We discussed an epidural. Karen remained noncommittal, letting us talk without offering advice. Meghan wrestled with her dreams of how the birth would unfold.

"This isn't what I planned, Mom. What do you think?"

"Take it," I said, "that's what it's there for."

"It's important for you to get some rest for the birth," Karen weighed in. "You've done a great job. After the epidural you can sleep."

Todd nodded his assent, relief flooding his face.

When the handsome Indian doctor came in, his black hair slicked back under a white cap, I felt a surge of terror. He was so young. How many times had he done this? I had heard stories of anesthesiologists missing the right point in the spine, of blowing it.

"You must hold completely still," he said to Meghan. Then he turned to Karen, "Can she do it?"

"Yes," Karen said. "She'll be fine."

The doctor shooed us all out, except for Todd who would hold Meghan from the front while the doctor placed the needle in her spine, and Karen who would assist.

I paced the tiny waiting room; now that there was nothing for me to do, fear and exhaustion seemed like a phantom body I carried piggyback. Ron and his wife watched TV. At last, I sat down. Ron looked over at me.

"I can't believe we did this without so much as an aspirin," I said. I didn't care that the current wife could hear. I was reaching back in time to grab the most important thing that Ron and I still had in common – the birth of our daughter. I said "we" because he had done it with me, coaching me, bringing me ice chips, leaning in behind Penny as she pressed on my belly and encouraged me to endure. Penny even let Ron deliver Meghan's body after she had finessed out the baby's head, which had seemed to me the size of a Halloween pumpkin.

"All right, Mr. Jones," Penny had said, stepping away. She was Scottish and a bit formal and ironic. "You take over now."

Ron caught his daughter as she slipped through my legs. There's a photo of him looking down at her, love and tears falling on her bare chest. I think that may have been the moment when our marriage unraveled for good. After that, he stopped his attentions to Maya, my older daughter from a previous marriage. So much of his affection went toward Meghan that what little passion was left in our erratic sexual life could not defuse the growing tensions in our blended family.

Now Ron tilted back in his plastic hair, shifting his weight. There was a brief flash of recognition in his eyes as if he too could see that hot August afternoon when Meghan was born in our bedroom on Pine Street in Nevada City. I sat across from him in the waiting room and fidgeted, praying the young doctor knew his business. At last, Karen came and called us back in to the room. I searched my daughter's face.

Meghan sat propped up by pillows on the bed, smiling. Todd held her hand, never taking his eyes from her face.

"So much better, Mommy," she said when I asked how she was. "I can't feel anything." She broke into a grin.

"Yaaaay," I said, the room's peach walls and gray laminate counters receding in a blur of relief. What I really wanted to do was drop to my knees and utter several million "Thank you Gods." Instead, I released a held breath in a long whistle and rubbed Meghan's shoulder.

Her father and stepmother came in. Karen assured them that everything was OK, and informed us that the birth might still be many hours away. Meghan was not fully dilated despite her mega-contractions, so Ron and Tatiana opted to go home. I lingered, not really trusting the medical assessment. If I had been one of the twelve apostles, I would have been Doubting Thomas, the one who put his hands in Christ's wounds just to be really *really* sure that Jesus had risen from the dead. I needed to see for myself that Meghan was pain-free.

I chatted with my daughter and son-in-law. I yawned. I must have looked like death warmed over. I had slept only a few hours the night before.

Finally, Meghan urged me to go home. I nodded, still unsure that this medical miracle would last.

"Are you sure?" I asked.

"Mom...." She gave me the "For God's sake!" look.

"Okay," I said, "I'll have the cell phone on. Call me if anything changes."

13

I kissed her forehead, gave Todd a hug, and backed away from the bed waving. When I stepped into the hallway, I remembered the bottle of very expensive Blanc de Blanc I had put in the hospital refrigerator that morning anticipating that the baby, which we had known for months would be a girl, would arrive that night. Hah! Well she would arrive eventually, and we'd drink our toast in *her* sweet time.

At the door to the waiting room, I paused. Was I abandoning my daughter in her hour of need? What if the baby was born before I could get back? Then I pictured my cushy bed and my cat Oliver waiting by the front door, and pushed my weary legs toward the parking garage.

* * * * *

Squinting at the clock face I read the green glow – six thirty. Jesus! I bounded up. Pale pink light seeped under the blinds. I checked my cell for messages. Nothing. I dialed Todd's cell. No answer. "Oh God," I said, and then chanted *oh god oh god oh god* as I stumbled to the bathroom. What if something had gone wrong?

When I realized I had not written down the phone number for Labor and Delivery, I went into overdrive. I phoned the Kaiser main number and asked to be connected. When someone picked up, I asked about my daughter. The voice on the other end said, "We can't give out any information about patients, I'm very sorry."

I panicked. How was I going to find out what was happening? Then I had a sudden inspiration. There had been a shift change right after the epidural and a lovely younger nurse named Sarah had replaced Karen. I had noticed that she often checked her cell phone.

"Can you give me Sarah's cell number please?"

The voice on the other end belonged to someone who was either a saint or an idiot. "Sure," it said, and delivered a string of numbers.

I tapped them into my cell keypad. One ring. Another. Then Sarah answered. A Lourdes-level miracle.

"It's Eleanor," I said, "Meghan's mom."

"We're delivering a baby," Sarah said. "By the looks of things, she'll be born in about twenty minutes."

I heard grunts and unintelligible syllables of exhortation.

"I'm on my way," I said. I bolted for my closet. No WAY was I going to miss the birth. I pulled on jeans and a sweater and raced to the car.

I fumbled with the key in the ignition, then whooped when the engine turned over. I was going to be a grandmother! That simple knowledge filled me with enough joy to lift a roomful of helium balloons out of earth's orbit.

But as I backed out of the garage and into the driveway, a realization slowly dawned. Todd knew I would call. Yet he didn't answer. I put the car in park and idled in the driveway, thinking. "Ohhhhhh," I said to my windshield. He could easily have called me back, but he hadn't. Did they want this moment to themselves?

I sat with hands folded in my lap, the engine humming, taking this in. I licked my lips and sighed. I knew in my heart of hearts that the moment belonged to them.

Slowly and carefully I put the car in reverse and backed out of my driveway, swinging onto Erie Street, then right onto Prince. At Lakeshore Avenue I paused and checked for oncoming traffic. Now that there was no rush I noticed that the sycamore trees had lost their leaves and there was a faint smell of wood smoke in the air. It was early on the morning of November 22nd, the Sunday before Thanksgiving. No one was out. I tapped the accelerator and rolled along until the car stopped on its own in front of my neighborhood Starbucks. Todd and I are both passionate about chai tea lattes. This tall thirty-four-year-old man with red-blonde whiskers is a former surfer who loves my daughter even more than he loves the ocean. Which means beyond words. Todd had introduced me to the "dirty chai," with an added shot of espresso to strengthen the Indian spices and foamy milk. I ordered a Grande dirty chai for him, a Tall nonfat plain chai for me, and a mocha for Meghan. Then I went next door to Noah's and bought a selection of bagels and two tubs of schmear.

By the time I reached the hospital, the sun was up. The dashboard clock read 7:50. As I pulled over the hill on Anza Street, I noticed a young woman in blue scrubs. It was Sarah going off shift.

I pulled over, rolled down the window, and yelled out her name.

She looked at me blankly for a few seconds and then broke into a wide grin. "You have a beautiful granddaughter," she shouted. "Meghan was amazing."

"Thank you!" I shouted back. "I can't thank you enough!" A waterfall of gratitude spilled over me. I parked the car and hurried in.

When I opened the door to Meghan's room, I saw my daughter's head bent over a tiny face. Meghan was wearing tortoise shell glasses and had her hair pulled back in a ponytail. Meghan gazed down at her new daughter snuggled against her breast. Todd's cheeks were bright pink with happiness.

"Hola!" I said, wrapping all my tenderness in a smile.

"Hola, Mimi," Todd greeted me. We had agreed that Mimi would be my grandmother name. When I heard it now, I knew it was right. I set the teas and the espresso on the bedside table. The bag of bagels smelled like sesame

15

seeds and yeast. I wiped my hands on my jeans and went to see my granddaughter.

"She's beautiful," I said looking down at the little moon face shining up at me from Meghan's arms. I stroked the baby's cheek and felt the amazing softness of new skin.

"Caffeine," Meghan said without taking her eyes off her daughter's face.

I extended the mocha. She took a sip and sighed with pleasure. Then she offered me her daughter.

I held my granddaughter next to my heart for the first time. She was tiny, amazingly pink, and smelled of warm flannel. Perfect.

Does heartbreak have an opposite? Crazy over-the-moon joy? Gratitude so deep it invites you to dive all the way to the bottom?

Meghan and Todd discussed names. They had agreed to wait and see the baby before deciding. Meghan liked Lucy – Todd hated it – but Meghan wanted a girl she could nickname Lu. Lucia was the compromise.

"She looks like a Lucia," I said. "Lu-see-ah," I crooned and her little mouth curved. I handed her back to Meghan.

"Lucia Maya Coleman," Meghan said, directing her words to her husband. "What do you think?"

"I like it," Todd said, gazing at his daughter's face.

Lucia Maya Coleman. I felt the honor Meghan was bestowing on her dead sister. I thought about how proud Maya would be of her brand new niece. And I wondered if the little bundle I had just handed over to her mother might have some spark of the impish little girl that Maya had been.

One human being cannot make up for the loss of another. I will never get Maya back. And yet Lucia's birth balanced the scales somehow. The deep longing to hold an infant connected by blood and bone, history and the quirks of personality, suddenly seemed fulfilled. My daughter had a daughter. And although Lucia was not "mine," she was as close to it as fierce love could make her.

* * * * *

After a year of slow dancing with grandmotherhood, my time as a mother has distilled into sweeter, less complicated love. My only job is to be present for Lucia.

The party for Lucia's first birthday was a boisterous gathering of family and friends packed into Meghan and Todd's third-floor shotgun flat in the inner Richmond. The steeple of the University of San Francisco glimmered golden in the pale November light. I held Lucia in my arms and gazed out the kitchen window across the rooftops.

Hard to imagine that she had been the little mite wrapped in a flannel blanket, eyes swollen as a newborn kitten, only twelve short months ago. Now she babbled and crawled with lightning speed. Just a few days ago she had taken her first steps.

Along with a set of wooden blocks, a "Good Night San Francisco" flip book, and a new sweater, I gave Lucia a gift I thought I would keep forever: Maya's little blue woolen coat and hat. For the last eighteen and a half years it had hung in the coat closet swathed in plastic. The smocked front with its double row of tiny white buttons, the tailored round collar, the way the pale blue wool hangs in neat gathers never fails to bring back the eighteen-month-old toddler who wore it on Easter Sunday in 1974. There's a snapshot of Maya tucked into the mirror by my front door, her white tights bagging at the knees, black patent leather shoes gleaming, her arm stretched forward pointing at the camera.

It's odd how the clothes of the dead still contain them – that coat makes my daughter's missing body real again. The aunt that Lucia will never know was nineteen when she died, the coat long outgrown, yet when I look at the expression on that little girl's face in a fading photograph, I see the young woman she would become, the verve and mischief in my little girl's eyes.

Elegant in slim black tights and a black and turquoise patterned dress, Meghan sat Lucia in a highchair festooned with balloons.

"Dat, dat, dat," Lucia babbled pulling the balloons to her with their long curly ribbons. "Dat" translates to "that," or as one friend joked, Lucia's first language is Dutch.

When Meghan placed a vegan cake with blueberry icing on Lucia's highchair tray and lit a chunky white candle in the shape of a numeral one, the baby seemed perplexed. But with one taste of cake, there was no stopping her. Within moments her lips were smeared purple.

We sang Happy Birthday and applauded Lucia. She made it through her first year. And Meghan and Todd survived the milestones – jaundice, the first tooth, the broken sleep, angry rashes, rolling over, sitting, crawling, and now their baby's first steps.

This spring it will be nineteen years since Maya died – she will have been gone for as long as I had her with me. Yet the way it felt to hold my daughters comes back to me every time I take Lucia in my arms and she puts her chubby hands around my neck. Loss and new life seesaw up and down in my heart, a giddy balance.

Sarah Brown Weitzman

Nothing For You

They're a bad lot here
and they hit me

And she thought they weren't feeding her
in the nursing home

Nothing for you
she said
they said
and sobbed
and could not be consoled

But I can go
when you go
Take my hand
and don't leave
without me

I signal the attendant
to distract her
so I can sneak away
to my own life

Take comfort
the doctor tells me
for the time being
at least
your mother still knows you

The Forgetting

It probably began as towers
of unread newspapers left to yellow

and crumble, or common nouns
misplaced, then piles of greengray stinks

in an unrepaired refrigerator, hundreds
of eggs hidden in the linen drawers

as my mother's memory faded my album Polaroids
though she knew me still as I sat beside her

in the nursing home holding her hand, feces
caked under her fingernails as she says:

"I had dogs a long time ago,"—
actually no more than three months

for here each of her days is as long as a month
in this white walled prison of her room and brain.

Tied to a chair she plans a picnic with her mother
dead for forty years, listing the foods I am to bring:

grape jelly slathered on ham, loin lamb chops, mashed potatoes
with mustard, cakes with brown gravy and lots, yes, lots of toast.

I try to play along but say all the wrong things. I tell her
that her favorite brother, dead now twenty years,

called to say hello to "Tootie," a nickname he gave her
when she was a child in Wilkes-Barre where sometimes

she thinks she is but then it is worse and she tries to slap me
with her one usable hand in her frustration to stand up and walk

away from "these people," the same hand that creamed
butter, eggs and sugar together and added flour and milk slowly

for a moist, heavy, yellow vanilla cake I've never mastered.
She doesn't remember the Japanese maple whose ruby branches arched

like an umbrella in the yard she let fall back into jungle
so that when the buyer took it over, he leveled all the trees

and horticultural treasures, a wild azalea, honeysuckle and grape vines,
black-eyed Susans tall as I am, a spread of Lily of the Valley up to the
fence,

even chopping down the great oak to run a circular driveway,
grassing over the narrow driveway between the fence and the house

that I hit once with my first car and my father stormed in a fury.
She doesn't remember any of this, not even the brook at the foot

of the hill that absorbed my attention for years with its changes
of flora and fauna and icy rushing in spring—so much to tell

of that childhood that I've forgotten my subject: my mother
in her agony of blankness, a bundle of limited reflexes and huge griefs.

But she does remember the poems of childhood learned at school
"Barbara Frietchie," Robert Louis Stevenson's "Shadows," and can still
sing

"Red Wing," but asks for her Betty constantly. That's me I tell her:
"I'm Betty." "Oh, yes, I know you are Betty but I want my little Betty."

She looks at me with horror when I explain that I'm her little Betty
now all grown up and she never asks again for Betty.

My mother's life ended in this gradual forgetting so I try to remember it,
putting it down in the constraint of couplets so I can hold it all in.

Measuring Spoons

Fanned out on the counter they resemble a family
of four in size place, their social ranks tattooed on

what equates to thighs: ¼, ½, tsp., tbsp.
Yet how perfectly they fit together

in corresponding convex or concave waves
back in the drawer. "Why don't I look like anybody?"

I used to rant, both parents handsome as film stars,
my mother's siblings like the proverbial peas in a pod,

my father's father and his three siblings all looking like brothers
of Spencer Tracy. My hair not Gilda but Little Orphan Annie red,

so short always the last to be chosen for any team,
I resembled no one on either side of the family

nor anyone in town where I was the only redhead
and where I felt like a new girl every September

when the other girls squinted and smirked as I walked by
and whispered or laughed so that my stomach drops

even now fifty years later when I overhear
giggling teens or when some sudden reminder like these

measuring spoons or a family group photo in a newspaper
jolts me anew with what I found out when I was thirty-two:

I'd been adopted.

Under the Yellow Ceiling

my mother is mixing a half-dozen muffins
this March evening. Tall in her high heels,

she creams the butter and sugar, then slowly adds
the eggs. She smells of Shalimar and vanilla

in the oven-warm kitchen. Intent, she doesn't speak
except about her own mother's cakes. I am

waiting as patiently as nine can for a heaping tablespoon
of batter for my jar-lid pan for a tiny cake of my own.

Still wearing his jacket and tie my father's reading
the newspaper. Through the glass door, we can see him

sitting in the big side-winged horsehair chair
in the bay window. We know he's waiting too

to read the war news to us as the house fills with the odor
of rising dough. Hiroshima is a name we don't know

yet. Outside the gloom sits on the porch settee
and whines like a dog to be left in.

Finally, it is time. My mother's muffins have billowed
high out of their cups, golden as the kitchen ceiling

and edged with a perfect complement of brown.
But my tiny cake, left in too long, is flat, rock-hard

and charred black. Oh, how I weep like a lost child
now for my childhood and that little ruined cake.

Jacqueline Kolosov

Re-reading Anna Karenina

"With a name like that, how can you not read Russian?" the Moscow writer asked during the reception dinner of an international conference devoted to the art of translation. I explained that my parents came from different countries and backgrounds; I stressed that excepting English, the common language in my family was German. Nevertheless, two weeks later the Moscow writer sent copies of his English prose and a single volume of poetry. In Russian. The inscription read: "To Jacqueline, who reads Russian in her soul."

How I wish that were true, especially now that my St. Petersburg-born grandmother is no longer alive to narrate stories from her own life as we sit sipping steeping cups of Assam tea in her living room. Without my grandmother, I must rely on Russia's writers, a few cherished artifacts, in particular a rose gold ring once buried in a wartime garden; and memory, to bring that necessary part of myself into being.

Of all the volumes in my well-fortified library, it is *Anna Karenina* that claims the central place. When I first read the novel, I was an eighteen-year-old freshman who had not yet declared her major at the University of Chicago (though that statement is not exactly accurate). Yes, my father dreamt of a daughter on Wall Street or in some famous firm with branches in at least three major European cities; a daughter who would begin to remake the family's lost fortune. But even then, I think I knew that I would study literature, having been in the habit of disappearing into other people's stories ever since my grandmother sat me down with the battered photo album containing images going all the way back to her childhood in St. Petersburg before the Revolution. And later came those golden schooldays when I spent every free afternoon tucked beneath the blankets, a cellophane-covered library book propped open on my belly.

Even so, looking back on my decision to enroll in Professor Wasiolek's graduate-level Tolstoy Course during my first year at Chicago, I question my motives and my self-confidence, not to mention the wisdom of the student advisor who typed my name into the computer registration. Wasiolek's syllabus slated *War and Peace, Anna Karenina*, and several shorter works including *The Death of Ivan Ilyich* for the ten week session. Nearly everyone in the class had read the novels before, and a good number had read them in Russian.

I managed to enroll, I suppose, because of my straight 'A' high school record in English, my naivety, and my desire to come a little bit closer to my father's family history, one I had always understood in epic terms. Perhaps as early as twelve or thirteen, I'd heard the story of my grandfather's first wife, a pianist, who threw herself into the Neva when she learned of her daughter's death in a bombing during the Second World War.

I also knew that my great-grandmother's sister Felicia had organized the killings of more than a dozen Bolsheviks (my father's term) responsible for her husband's murder. That's right. After she gave the signal—a particular tune she played upon the piano, a favorite tune she would never again play afterwards—the Ukrainian partisans opened fire on her house which the Bolsheviks had taken over.

Having planned everything down to the last detail, Felicia fled the country with two horses. Over the course of five days, she managed to make it across the border and into Lithuania where there was still a family house, though it was now in ruins. Felicia swam rivers with those horses. And when she slept, it was always deep within the shelter of the trees.

These stories, nearly all of which were distinguished by the family's women and not by its military men, have everything to do with why I dedicated myself to the art of the story. And what better way to learn about stories, especially Russian stories, than a class on Tolstoy taught by a scholar whose name reverberated through the university's hallowed halls?

I arrived on time for every lecture held in a cozy seminar room in Harper Library. Here, the windows were of leaded glass, and many of us sat on the floor, for the class was surprisingly crowded, but then again, this *was* Chicago; though the Russian woman with waist-length blonde hair and blue, almond-shaped eyes like one of the icons in the Russian Orthodox Church my grandmother would take me to at Christmas time, never joined us on the floor. No, her ankle-length velvet skirts with their elaborate embroidery were far too beautiful for the dusty wood; and her expressive voice, far too serious and sad.

My back ached all through that winter because I spent almost every night in one of the green chairs on the mildew-scented fourth floor of Regenstein Library. Curled up in a chair big enough to seat two of me, I felt a little bit like Alice, had she stepped into nineteenth century Russia in winter. There may not have been an onion-domed cathedral in the distance, or a czar in the palace; but there was gothic architecture at the University of Chicago, and it was incredibly cold, and there was snow on the ground, with daylight ending shortly after five p.m. On those star-sharp nights, I'd go down to the basement cafeteria every two hours or so and order sweet black tea from the vending machine, then sneak it back upstairs by tucking the hot Styrofoam cup in my sleeve.

Almost twenty years later, I picked the novel up again because the gray cold, such a rare thing in West Texas where I now live, brought back that extraordinary winter at Chicago; but also because the Moscow writer's atmospheric stories have enabled me to see again the pristine snow shining beneath the fabled cities of Moscow and St. Petersburg, cities my grandparents once walked through; cities I long to see.

I opened *Anna Karenina* and read until the waning moon glittered like a faraway Fabergé gem. Until I arrived at Tolstoy's rendering of Anna's time in Italy with Vronsky. Chapter Eight of Part Five is one of the first and only sections where Tolstoy gives the reader any real access to Anna's happiness. Most of the time, Anna, despite her love for Vronsky, is unhappy.

"Anna," Tolstoy tells us, "in that first period of her emancipation...felt herself unpardonably happy....The memory of all that had happened....seemed like a delirious dream, from which she had awakened abroad and alone with Vronsky....The more she got to know Vronsky, the more she loved him....In everything he said, thought, did, she saw something particularly noble and elevated....She dared not show him her feeling of inferiority beside him. It seemed to her that, knowing this he might sooner cease to love her; and she dreaded nothing now so much as losing his love..."

Reading this passage now, I cannot help but criticize Tolstoy for commingling Anna's fear of her unworthiness with her love for that lesser being, Vronsky. To the shrewd reader I've become, Anna is without any doubt the nobler, braver spirit. Amazing that I did not see this before when Tolstoy plants the evidence of her superiority everywhere!

In Chapter Twenty-two of Part Four, for example, the pair meets in a secluded garden. Vronsky, not Anna, fears their discovery by a group of approaching ladies—ladies, for god sakes—and cries out, "'Perhaps they know us!'" But Anna says, "'Oh, I don't care!'" Even more revealing is Vronsky's own perception that at that moment "[Anna's] eyes looked at him from under the veil with strange anger." Isn't Anna's muted fury a sign that she expects her lover to rise to her level, that of a woman who has given up everything for him?

The only way Tolstoy could have redeemed or at least allowed the woman I have become to enter into Anna's dream, howsoever delusional, would have been by giving me access to it. Yes, yes, I know, not even the greatest of the nineteenth century Russian novelists would have dared to give the reader Anna's sexual awakening. Such things, I have learned from Chekhov,

Turgenev, nearly all of the major English novelists, and the essential Goethe, were not done before the twentieth century.

But the eighteen-year-old girl who spent a week reading *Anna Karenina* in a library's oversized armchair, the sleeves of her sweaters stained by tea, her back chafed by radiator heat, did not disbelieve Anna's delirious happiness. Twenty years ago I understood very little about sex. Despite my thrift shop chic and habit of appropriating seductive lines from actresses like Bette Davis and Julie Christie, I remained an inexperienced girl with a history of succumbing to hopeless or at least absurd crushes; first at sixteen when I was living for the summer in Nürnberg and shared my lemon yellow umbrella with an American boy who loved, not me, but baseball and a cheerleader back home named Penelope. That first term at Chicago, there was Mark, the petal-skinned, bohemian art history student who wore a beret and was probably gay. Come winter, the object of my affection was skinny, sorrel-eyed James from Philadelphia who spoke an alternative rock lingo peppered with beginning astrophysics that I mistook for genius. When I took James home for Thanksgiving, he went out for ice cream with my fifteen-year-old sister. Shouldn't I have taken that as a sign?

For the eighteen-year-old me, *Anna Karenina* was sophistication of the vicarious University of Chicago kind. Eight hundred pages long with an admirable and extremely beautiful heroine, a tragic ending in keeping with the atmosphere of the stories my grandmother told, and that illustrious Russian pedigree.

And yet, looking back, I realize there really was risk involved in my reading. Not sexual risk, but intellectual risk, the only kind I understood. And that winter, for the first time in my life, I was no longer too smart for my own good. In fact, in Wasiolek's class I was suddenly not smart enough, for I earned a 'B-' in that class.

Seven years passed before I picked *Anna Karenina* up again. I was now a newly married bride with a Tiffany wedding ring and eight place settings of elegantly simple Queen Anne silver. But although I believed myself "a woman of the world," I continued to make my home in the bookstore-lined enclave of Hyde Park.

Is it significant, I wonder now, that I met my husband, Alex, immediately after that winter quarter devoted to Tolstoy? I have no way of knowing how my life might have unfolded had I not married the man with whom I first fell head over my penny loafer-ed heels in love...

Alex may have shared his first name with my great-grandfather, but he wasn't Russian but Scottish on his father's side and Dutch English on his mother's. He was an American History major three years my senior. I admired his steep forehead and his brooding blue eyes, not to mention his height and the rumpled distraction of his Brooks Brothers clothes. And in his tales of travels to Italy, Scotland, Ireland and the Swiss Alps, I recognized an adventurous dreamer's spirit like my own. On our first date Alex took me to a tenth floor Chinese restaurant with a balcony overlooking Hyde Park. It was April, and the weather was so mild I wore only a thin sweater over my jeans. Standing on that balcony with the neighborhood lights twinkling below, I drank two martinis, for the second time in my life. (The first time was on the exchange students' trip to Berlin with the baseball-loving boy who shared my umbrella.)

After talking well into the early morning hours, I fell asleep on the floor of Alex's room wearing all my clothes and my loafers. The next week, he took me to see Haley's comet at the observatory, and all through that spring he accompanied me on long runs along the lakefront and embraced my passion for reading at the beach on balmy summer afternoons. Thanks to him, I learned to love Bob Dylan, jazz, and the Rolling Stones. Thanks to me, he learned to dance with rhythm and to learn to like vegetarian cuisine. A year into our relationship, we rucksack-ed our way through Germany and Austria, then splurged on an automobile and drove to the south of France. Six years later, we were married at the university's Rockefeller Chapel while he earned a doctorate in Theological Ethics and I finished my Masters degree in English.

I returned to *Anna Karenina* on a snowy day in December a few days after we toasted our first anniversary with a bottle of vintage champagne. I was running a very high fever, and the only thing I could do was lie in bed in the tulip pink room with the lead glass windows, and read. And what better book than the novel I'd read at eighteen and could only tenuously remember, having crammed its epic proportions into the space of two weeks?

By this time, though still naïve, I was at least coming a little closer to the Anna of Tolstoy's novel. By this time, I knew what it was to be deliriously happy with a man. Of course, in Anna's case that man is not her hierarchical, intensely class-conscious husband; a man wedded to the inky letter and not to the winged spirit of the law. And in Anna's case, even in her happiest moments, as we saw in that chapter in Italy, there remains foreboding, for after painting such a contented albeit grateful portrait of Anna during the lovers' brief stay in Italy, Tolstoy reveals that Vronsky "was not perfectly happy." Like Anna, Vronsky, too, has sacrificed something. Not the respectability of marriage and the precious love of a child. No, what Vronsky has sacrificed is his career. Why does the reader finds him painting in an atelier in the neglected old palazzo in which the lovers live? For the exiled Vronsky, painting must take the place of profession. Meanwhile, Anna must sit for her portrait, but she cannot pick up the artist's brush.

A year into our marriage, neither Alex nor I had made any real sacrifices for an intellectually expansive way of life. True, I paid for my Masters degree using a student loan and the ten thousand dollars I'd managed to save while working at the university press. But Alex had a trust fund which paid for our apartment in a turn of the century cooperative just two blocks from the university. That trust fund also paid for our European honeymoon and later, for the apartment we rented on New York's Upper West Side when I earned a doctoral fellowship at NYU.

As my temperature escalated, I imagined my way into identification with Tolstoy's heroine, embracing neither suffering nor her sacrifice, but her radiance, that quality that holds all—not just men but women also—in thrall. And why not when I had at last grown into my long-limbed, lanky body and had even discovered how to make my nearsightedness appealing.

The second time Anna meets Vronsky, she is at a ball, and it is through the younger and virtuous Kitty's eyes that Tolstoy allows the reader to see her. "Kitty had been seeing Anna every day; she adored her....now, seeing her in black, she felt that she had not fully seen her charm. She saw her now as someone quite new and surprising.... [Anna's] black dress, with its sumptuous lace, was not conspicuous on her; it was only the frame, and all that was seen was she—simple, natural, elegant, and at the same time gay and animated."

Though the memory of that feverish time has grown faint, I still recall a waking dream in which I waltzed at a ball wearing a décolleté black dress, a strand of pearls just like Anna Karenina's encircling my throat, my own Siberian blue eyes shining with the possibilities that seemed to open up before me. For the girl-woman I was at twenty-five, *Anna Karenina* meant desirability and possibility. But equally important, the novel seemed to bring me a little bit closer to the rich tapestry of my family history.

And what did that history involve? My Moscow-born grandfather's arrival at the opera where, my grandmother and later my father told me with all the sorrowing desire of the exile, he heaped bouquet after bouquet of roses into the arms of glistening divas, then dined at a fashionable club dressed in the turn-of-the-century equivalent of black tie. In the old Russia, there was even a statue of my great-grandfather in some Moscow public square. My father searched for it when he visited the city for the first time three years ago, only to realize that it must have been torn down...

My great-grandfather was a high ranking military official in charge of Russia's most prestigious academy who chose to flunk a lazy Romanov cousin of the czar rather than compromise his standards. Despite the polished bronze of his father's example, my own grandfather broke with family tradition and became a structural engineer. A builder of bridges. And despite the fact that the story of their meeting is now lost, just before the Revolution my grandfather married the pianist from whom he became separated during 1917. A woman I have tried to imagine countless times, infusing her hair with the fragrance of lilies; and picturing her always with her daughter's large, dark eyes; all the while wondering what piece of music she most loved to play.

My grandmother, the niece of the courageous Felicia, was the only daughter of a three star general. In St. Petersburg my grandmother attended the Empress Catherine's School for Girls. In a surviving photograph I keep in a well-polished silver frame on my desk, my grandmother wears white ribbons in her hair, as do all of the other immaculately dressed little girls. My grandmother, who was fifteen years her husband's junior, was still a round-cheeked child when her family fled Russia. Instead of completing her St. Petersburg education and debuting at a candlelit event where a white-gloved young man kissed her hand then asked her to waltz through a gleaming ballroom, my grandmother spent her teenage years on a farm in Lithuania. During the war years, she and her family ate potatoes and hung rugs on the walls for warmth; and when the marauding soldiers drew near, they buried their jewelry and other valuables in a plot behind the house.

Later came flight across barbed wire borders after nightfall. Bombings. Hunger. The loss of home, friendship, family. What became of Felicia and her mother's seven other siblings, my grandmother never knew. And the pianist's dark-eyed daughter who died during a bombing? She was also my grandfather's child. Her name, my grandmother told me only once, was Galena.

Six months after my fever ended, *Anna Karenina* once more restored to my well-dusted shelf, I awoke to my husband's belief that twenty years had passed. And no, he did not have a fever. Instead, with wide, amazed eyes he stroked my cheek and told me how young I looked. Then he began to weep.

When I tried to console him—believing that he had been startled out of that strange sort of dream that somehow remains all too real even after waking—his mood swung to the opposite pendulum, and I heard him accuse me of having an affair with his best friend in the divinity school, a Xaverian missionary and an ordained priest in the Roman Catholic Church.

The girl-wife who imagined herself in the candlelit whirl of a ballroom now walked with my young husband to the emergency room at the University of Chicago Hospital. After Alex was examined by a very conscientious resident whose hazel eyes held my own for a long time as if she held my future there— if only I knew how to read it—she signed the papers that admitted him to the psychiatric ward. By the second day, the doctors had made the diagnosis. Like his father's twin sister, Alex was diagnosed with bipolar disorder, an illness characterized by manic highs and catastrophic lows. "The mania's been building for weeks now," the hazel-eyed resident said, stunned that I had not registered the change.

I did not know how to tell her that even if there had been clues—the paranoid thinking, the phenomenal intellectual leaps, the belief that Chicago would hire him before he completed his PhD—the girl-wife I was didn't know how to read them. The signs may have been there—and here I think of Vronsky's exquisite-eyed mare lost through his careless riding, her death a pre-figuration of Anna's own—but what do signs mean without a way of understanding them?

Alex spent three and a half weeks in the psychiatric ward. I visited every day, arriving with small gifts and believing, despite the way he fell in love with his nurse and alternately adored and shunned me, he and I would be able to go back to the enchanted life of before. An un-awakened life.

What did I do while he was hospitalized? I took long, hot baths; and I read, though the novels weren't Russian or tragic. No, the novels of that un-tethered summer included Frances Burney and all I had not yet read or carefully re-read of Jane Austen. Neatly executed British novels where tea and buttery cakes are served at three o'clock sharp, the lamps lit at six, and the lavender-scented beds turned down at ten. Novels where men and women make intelligent but almost always polite conversation and marry, at least for the most part, within their social class…

During the next six years, my education involved learning how to distinguish what I fiercely hoped to see through half-closed eyes from what was actually there. And what did I hope to see? A lucid, talented husband who would go on to find a position in a respected theology department while I completed my doctorate, then found an equally fine position. But underlying the professional success, what I most hoped to see was a stable life enlivened by friends and eventually by children; a life in which hardship would mean car repairs, breaks with friends, the occasional illness, losses of loved ones to old age; but never delusion, mania, paranoia, or the heart-sick well of depression.

But as Alex's daily existence and my own was ensnared by drugs and psychiatrists and his new need for a highly structured life which led him away from the tenuous but provocative field of religious ethics and into the more stable and more regimented life of the ministry (a new career he began during three years of study at the Princeton Theological Seminary), I felt my vision of who we were and would be slipping further and further away. Three years after he and I walked home from the psychiatric ward, I found myself seated opposite a psychologist who asked me what I wanted, and who I was apart from being Alex's wife, and I could not answer her…

Is it enough to say that unlike Anna Karenina, dear Anna who Tolstoy abandons after conjuring her graceful, exquisite person into being, I eventually made the decision to walk away from a marriage I entered into with the bright-eyed naivety of a smart, protected, well-disciplined girl? And therein returns the connection. Anna would have been infinitely better off had she read the French philosophers as well as the French novelists, before she met Vronsky. But Anna's *bildung* did not include novels. Instead, it is loneliness and the loss of her position that transforms her into a reader.

Rereading *Anna Karenina* now, I find myself mapping out the distance I have traveled since I first sat down with the novel in a library chair. I'm no longer a girl who falls in love with men whose beautiful gestures or habits—disheveled clothes, brooding blue eyes—can become the raw material of a desired ideal. Nor am I one who believes so unquestioningly in love that I convince myself I can sacrifice anything for it. I now understand the costs of sacrifice, but equally important I understand the costs of betrayal.

I now see that Anna betrayed herself in loving Vronsky. Twenty years after my first reading, it is the following revelation made shortly before Anna leaves her life in Russia for the promise of Italy and Vronsky that has captured my attention. "She laid her hands on [Vronsky's] shoulders, and looked a long while at him with a profound, passionate, and at the same time searching look. She was studying his face to make up for the time she had not seen him. She was, every time she saw him, comparing the picture she painted of him in her imagination (incomparably superior, impossible in reality) with him as he really was."

How can it be that it has taken me all these years to recognize the ways in which Anna blinded herself? After rereading my earlier annotations in the yellowing pages of my Modern Language Edition, I find nothing written here. And perhaps this realization is a good thing for it means that I've at last become smarter than the woman who lingered in an unhappy marriage. Because of those vows, yes. But also because it was safe.

Until the desire to see my own face in a more radiant light propelled me into adultery. If one speaks according to the letter and not the spirit of the law, by the time I fell in love with someone else, Alex and I no longer rolled up the Oriental rug and danced to Bob Dylan in the hours after midnight. Nor did we lean close together over a café table, our knees touching, and talk about the parallels between Virginia Woolf and Alfred North Whitehead.

No, having finished his studies at Princeton Theological Seminary, Alex had begun preaching to a congregation each Sunday in a small town in the Midwest. Initially, I tried to sit in the narrow Presbyterian pew with the eyes of the parishioners upon me, but I felt as if my own faith were on display, and I quickly found reasons not to attend; reasons Alex never questioned

31

outright, though his brooding eyes began to look at me, not with tenderness but with disappointment.

The red and gold leaves of that first Ohio autumn fell to the ground only to be buried beneath a heavy snowfall. As winter's cold stillness intensified, I lived increasingly in a world centered on reading, writing and teaching. Soon, not only was I working at a private college four days a week, but I was making the ninety-minute-drive to and from Bowling Green University two days a week to teach a night class in women's life writing.

Alex and I still ate the occasional dinner together, though our leisurely conversations over wine had long since ceased because his medications prohibited alcohol. As for walking or running side by side through twilight's streets, as we once had, I now walked or ran alone. And on too many nights I woke to a racing heart, my shoulders and neck bathed in sweat. On those nights, I stared at the moon through the lace-curtained windows and worried about my marriage until I no longer believed that vows and memories could make up for the breathless grief of the here and now.

The man with whom I fell in love possessed blue-gray eyes and a passion for birds and writing, and his daily life in a state far from my own enabled me to create the version of him that I needed. Yes, like Tolstoy's heroine, *I needed to paint an intoxicating picture in my imagination* to begin to realize a new vision of myself. By the time I boarded a plane and flew from my snowy home to visit my lover in a sun-drenched, though arid landscape, Alex had moved into an apartment belonging to the church, and we had initiated the drawn-out paperwork involved in divorce.

But unlike Anna, I did not wind up beneath the crushing wheels of a train. How could I, given the examples of women like my great aunt Felicia, and especially my grandmother who survived Revolution, two world wars, and an Atlantic crossing to the United States where she worked in the assembly line of a Chicago lamp factory and continued to ration her small indulgences of coffee, music, and new stockings as she had done throughout the war years, for by this time frugality had become a habit with her?

And through it all, my grandmother, once a white-ribboned schoolgirl standing beside a dark-eyed teacher in a St. Petersburg classroom, carried with her the family's few remaining jewels, treasures set in Russian rose gold she watched her own grandmother bury in the countryside; treasures she eventually willed to me...

I've reread many sections of the novel during this gray but not truly wintry December. But it is only the chapter centered on the mare's death that has made me weep. Because the mare trusts a man who miscalculates what he needs to do when she makes the most dangerous jump. Because he doesn't merit her trust, for when she jumps—instead of losing his seat in the saddle—Vronsky stays on. And because he stays on, he breaks the mare's back. And when she falls, initially he thinks only of his own dishonor. "With a face hideous with passion... Vronsky kicked her with his heel in the stomach and again began tugging at the rein. She did not stir, but thrusting her nose into the ground, she simply gazed at her master with speaking eyes....[until] for the first time in his life...[Vronsky] knew the bitterest sort of misfortune, misfortune beyond remedy, misfortune his own fault."

Marriage is an act of trust, and I betrayed Alex long before I left him. But wouldn't the greater betrayal have been to keep my seat in the saddle? Had I stayed, I would have stayed without loving him as a wife must love a husband. And that would have destroyed us both.

In *Anna Karenina*, Levin alone embodies the hard-won gift of standing outside himself and looking in at his life as if it were just a tiny, shining star in a vast, all too often incomprehensible universe... Not surprisingly Levin has the last word in *Anna Karenina*. It is nighttime, and Levin is standing in the garden and staring up at the stars. When his wife, the lovely Kitty, joins him, she smiles, and for a moment Levin believes she understands him, though her practical request makes clear that she does not. When Levin realizes that she is a world away, he does not fault Kitty. Instead, he understands that despite the fact that "'I shall go on in the same way, losing my temper... expressing my opinions tactlessly... blaming her for my own terror, and being sorry for it...[my life] has an unquestionable meaning of the goodness which I have the power to put into it.'"

Twenty years after first reading *Anna Karenina*, it is this discovery of the power of infusing my own life with goodness—despite all that I cannot possibly control within myself and without—that I, like Levin, claim for myself. Tonight, twenty years after my first reading, with my grandmother's diamond ring glinting within my lamp's rose gold circle of light, I find myself seeking again the violet-softened room overlooking her beloved garden. My grandmother, I believe, is waiting for me. After setting down her tea cup, she will reach for my hand. Our blue eyes will meet, and she will tell me that despite the smallness of my life's star, despite or perhaps because of all that I have lost, I remain her granddaughter. A woman who speaks Russian in my soul.

Mac Greene

A Life in 100 Words

1948   F… you, polio!!   **I'll walk.**

love?   PROBLEM CHILD   dad's belt

Mrs. Friedberg discovers my intelligence.   **books**   wallllllllllk

An Intellectual among Good Time Charleys

BOOKS   HIPPPEEeeeeeeeeeeeeeee!!!

hiking   My sons: 1969, 1971   I learn to love.

14 cabs and a garage   **books**   **birdwalks**

"I'll never marry a grease monkey."   my Ph.D./her M.D.

We fake it till we make it.

clinicalpsychologist/pediatric endocrinologist

DC -> Philly -> Wisconsin -> Indianapolis

More kids: 1989, 1990, 1994, 1994

gardening   **family eco-tourist treks**

Is it normal to be normal?

(secret hypochondriasis of aging)

2011

walking meditation

how many books on my bedside table?

34

Mariangela Mihai

Balcony

I. Balcony

The balcony of our one-bedroom apartment, on the fourth concrete story of the last building built in town, where the paved street abruptly stopped and the wild woods started, is the clearest image I have of my childhood. It is where I spent all of my time, whenever it was possible. For most of the year, the space was open to rain, snow and wind, but the few weeks of spring and the two months of summer were delightful.

On that balcony we dried our clothes, stored the trash, and kept secret from our neighbors the few items of "delicatessen" we managed to gather during the year: mostly pickled mushrooms, dried and smoked meat, and a few wooden boxes of apples wrapped in newspaper, and buried in sand. Actually, after all, it might have been the dungy moldy basement where we kept all that. Nevertheless, there was always some food on the balcony that I was not supposed to touch.

A wooden chair sat quietly in one corner. Apparently my great-grandfather, sometimes in his late eighties, made the chair in his shop at his house in the country side, then carried it on his back on a ten-hour trip, as a gift for my mom and dad's new life. It was the very year I was born. I never met him; he died two weeks before I decided that life in the womb was not satisfying anymore.

I never sat on the chair. It was more symbolic than functional, and somehow I understood that without being told. I'd usually bring a blanket from inside, drop it on the balcony's cold concrete floor, and make believe it was the softest sofa—softer than the luxurious linings on the immense beds described by Scheherazade in *One Thousand and One Nights*. I cannot recall why I had been given that book, but I know I enjoyed it immensely. It was colorful (in a literary sense), and its myriad colors, smells, and sounds came in handy in the black-and-white life we were all forced to live back then.

The balcony had its own will. It rejected strangers. Whenever we would have guests in our small room, I'd retreat on my balcony hoping that no one would come to share the space. I had balcony jealousy, and they must have known it. Thus, most people would come out only to resolve a few minutes later that "This balcony is too high, and open, and it makes me dizzy; I better go inside." Victory!

Now that I think about it, I am amazed I never fell off that balcony. After all, I played plenty of dangerous games, hanging by its edge. Once I even passed from our balcony to the neighbor's balcony, and back, only to see if I could. I didn't like theirs; it was empty, and somehow colder than mine. The balconies were separated only by a thin cardboard sheet, with a 20 cm gap right on the outside edge. There must have been about seventy meters between me and the ground, but back then I wasn't yet afraid of heights.

My friends would come up on my balcony sometimes, and we would play games. My favorite was throwing plastic bags filled with water on by passers. To most Romanians, swearing is an art. I loved helping some of them exercise that craft. I have been fascinated with language ever since I started talking. I remember sometimes looking in the mirror and talking to myself, only to see how the mouth moves when certain words are voiced. What can I say? I am an only child, and I never had imaginary friends. So, I played a bunch of corky games all by myself.

One evening, my favorite toy flew off that balcony. It was a small washing machine, with batteries and a motor that made an annoying noise, a loud buzz. I played with it all night, and all day. We didn't have a real washing machine (nor did we know anyone who did), so I pretended to help mom with her loads. Washing clothes was a real pain, and it always made her ill for days. When I didn't do homework or read a book, I played with my pretend washing machine. One day, my dad put his book aside, got up from bed, grabbed it, went to the balcony, and threw it off. No previous complaints, no asking me to stop, no warnings, nothing. I didn't cry, nor did I protest in any way.

I simply put my shoes on, made the dreadful trip on the total of eighty-eight steps connecting the four stories, went out and looked for my toy in semi darkness. I found it, checked if it worked, and brought it back upstairs. Nothing back then was made to last. It's not that Romanians didn't know how to make things; I simply think they didn't care. Communism does that to people: it makes them numb. But this little metal washing machine survived, and it remained until today one of the most durable things I remember from childhood. The walls collapsed, the doors fell on us, the roads didn't last long, the clothes thread apart too fast, our hopes were fading more and more, but my toy lived many years after it flew from the cuckoo's nest. Dad never touched it again. He laughed at me when I brought it back, said he was sorry, then all was forgotten.

Great-Grandpa's wooden chair didn't make it, though. I watched gravity work its magic, and marveled at the symmetry of its thousands of splinters scattered on the ground. I was glad mom didn't make the jump after all, after she screamingly announced it to my dad (who was trying to hold her), and to the neighbors who synchronously came out on their own balconies to see whatever happened. No one said "Don't jump," though the building facing ours was close enough to throw packets of cigarettes from one another, which some people sometimes did. Some watched the spectacle while smoking. Mom kept screaming and laughing in turns.

My dad didn't say, "Don't jump" either; he just said "Get inside, woman, it's getting late and I have to go to work." So she did, after she threw a few things off the balcony: her blouse, Scheherazade and all of her Arabian nights, one jar of pickled green tomatoes, a small box of potatoes, a hammer Dad borrowed from our next door neighbor, a few newspapers, and great grandpa's chair.

Dad carried Mom inside, and I stayed on the balcony for a few more minutes to look at the neighbors. No one said anything to me, nor to each other. They would all come out at the same time on their balconies only on a few occasions: when there was a game of soccer between the blocks, when there was a game of soccer on the radio, and when some crazy neighbor decided to announce she wanted to jump off her 4th story balcony.

The times they—and I—enjoyed the most was when Constantine, the funniest drunk in town, came out to swear at everyone for not lending him a cup of sugar, or for some other such petty reason. Constantine mastered his art, and entertained us once a month at least. He certainly earned his sugar. Sugar was rare back then, so any time we, the kids, would get hold of it, we'd spread it on a piece of bread and eat it like that.

Seeing Mom's face was rare too, after the scene on the balcony.

When I finally got back inside, Dad was holding my Mom's head in his palms, and she was crying—I think. The whole scene was dead silent and I couldn't tell if either of them was still breathing. I was sent down stairs to see if I can find the neighbor's hammer or any of our potatoes; we still needed those.

"Michaela, why did you have to throw the chair?" Dad asked on a soft voice, as I closed the door behind me.

I did find the potatoes, but someone took the neighbor's hammer.

II. Weekend visits.

"Voila" was a famous loony bin, filled with political prisoners, and rarely with genuine cases of insanity. Except for the spelling, there was nothing French about it. My father's uncle Nikki was a psychiatrist there. He eventually became the Director. He was an intelligent and refined man, and my dad wanted me to be like Uncle Nikki when I grew up. He had a car, which he called "Froggy," but in Romanian. Uncle Nikki was funny, generous, kind, and loved classical music.

37

Mom was "thriving" there, or that's what she always said when we visited. The food was horrible—Dad and I agreed, after mom let us taste it. Mom said "It's ok; Uncle Nikki sends me real food at least once a day, straight from his wife's kitchen." A nurse came in, and gave mom the noon pills. Mom drank a lot of water with them. After the nurse left, mom took them out from under her tongue and handed them to Dad, along with few others, stored in a napkin, hidden between a heating pipe and the wall. Dad took them, and hid them in his pocket. She smiled, and we all held hands as we walked the grounds.

I always wondered how come a place so sad and strange, with a tired, cold and desolated feeling to it, could have such beautiful grounds: atop a beautiful hill, with the majestic view of the Carpathian Mountains, and a crisp blue sky with perfectly shaped clouds within arms' reach.

We visited every Sunday, for many months. Dad and I got up in the morning before the roosters did, we took a train, then a bus, then we walked for awhile, and then we waited in a room. For a long time, Dad always said the waiting wasn't more than twenty minutes, but it felt like days. Eventually a very sad nurse saw us in the women's building.

"Voila" was not a loony bin, it was a prison. The first I've seen, with real bars, and all…

Everyone there was very skinny and always busy. Especially the patients: if they were not crying, they were screaming, swearing, begging, threatening, or asking for help. The nurses were busy too, but somewhere else. With the exception of the "noon-pills" incidents, and showing us in and out, I only recall seeing the doctors and the nurses running between buildings as if there was always something on fire.

My uncle knew my mother was not taking her pills; he knew she gave them all to Dad, on Sundays. He recommended it. My uncle knew more than I did about why she was there; he knew she didn't really want to die.

It wasn't that she needed time away from herself; she needed time away from others, dad told me one day when we were coming back from seeing her.

She needed time from others…

"From us?" I asked.

"No," Dad said without explaining.

"Don't ask too many questions, you are too small." Then he added: "It's not that I do not trust you, or that you could not understand, it's just that some things are better off not talked about."

I trusted him too, so I never asked again. Dad pushed Mom on a swing every Sunday. They laughed sometimes, and we all held hands.

Sandy pushed me on the swing. Sandy, my first boyfriend (or so I thought), came there every Sunday to see his dad. His dad was a doctor, a real doctor, but he did not work there. "He's here for his headaches," Sandy told my dad the first day we met. But later, dad whispered in my ear that Sandy's dad was hiding from the commies; that he did something good for others, but very bad for himself.

Sandy was many years older than I was (he must have been in his twenties), but he kissed my right cheek every time the swing would return to him to push again. He brought me chocolate sometimes, and smooched my hair. His hair was sandy, his eyes were green.

Mom eventually came home. She never threatened to jump from the 4th floor again, nor did we live so high anymore. We moved to the first floor. She was really sorry about great grandpa's chair.

Dad said "Forget it." And so we did.

Kristin Laurel

The Burn Unit

> *"…let us be shaken, let us be thankful, and so worship God acceptably with awe and reverence, for our God is a consuming fire."* Hebrews 12:29

I burn vanilla candles,
watch the soapsuds crackle and dissolve on my skin.
There's no smell of burnt flesh in my bathroom.

> Back in the tank room-
> bodies lie on metal tubs
> and hoses hang from the ceiling like a human car wash.

I was younger then, but I can still hear them…

Sophie was six years old,
raped, and then held down in boiling water
to cover up the sin.

She cried *Jesus, Jesus* as I
bathed her in pink Hibiclens, debrided the dead
skin, until she bled.

I applied the white salve of Silvadene,
got lost in the wrapping, hid in each square of fine mesh gauze,
until we finished. And then, she hugged me.

Old Charlie, sat in his boxers, covered his aching legs in rubbing alcohol,
then dropped his lit cigar in his lap. He told bad jokes
during his dressing change.

I apply more warm water before they shiver,
the ones on ventilators can't cry.
I wrap legs, arms, fingers, chests,

the cracks of buttocks, labia majoras,
swollen scrotal sacks. I've unwrapped
Thomas, gently, for the past three months;
his wounds kept getting infected.
After his Christmas tree and house caught fire,
he went back in to save his wife and kids, but

came out the sole survivor.

Donna suffered from depression.
She stood on the side of the highway,
poured a can of gasoline over her head, and

lit a match.

She stood there, consumed in flames, until
a passerby stopped, pushed her to the ground,
and threw a blanket over her to put her out.

She's spent over nine months in the hospital.
Over 90% of her body was burned.
She will tell you, through a bright crack

in her one un-contracted eye, sipping Ensure through a straw
in a pea sized mouth, pressing the can firmly between crisscrossed stubs,
because she has no hands,

that she is happy to be alive,
that she saw God that day,
and I tell you - you would believe her.

It didn't take long to look past

melted noses, missing lips, lost cartilage from an ear.
Some wore clear plastic masks on their faces
and thick Jobst stockings to lessen the scars.

Nothing good can come from burns
a friend tells me, while chugging ice cold beers...*I don't see how you work
there,* but I reply- *it's not to see the pain, it's to see the healing.*

41

I have come to fear ethanol glycol, bonfires, lightning strikes, dried up
Christmas trees, faulty wiring, fireworks, gasoline, hot grease, the heat of
the flame,
but not God.

> I was younger then and I saw suffering, yet
> I believed, I bore witness, I saw—
> the Holy Human Spirit.

Jasminne Mendez

I Miss You

I remember having dreams once. I remember believing in the impossible. I remember being someone else once. I was once a girl who dreamed big and a woman who always wanted more. Since my diagnosis however, I don't know where she went. I think she's died in this grueling process known as treat, recover, relapse, and repeat. I've lost HER somewhere. I tried to blame the illness, Scleroderma. I tried to blame God. But it's no one's fault. *She* couldn't take the pressure anymore. So *she* left.

The old me broke up with the new me and left the both of us broken-hearted. Imagine that, feeling the broken heart of two people at one time beating in your own chest. Grief becomes inevitable, depression a necessity.

I used to long for the old me, like every lover does at the beginning of a separation. I went back to her time and time again. I begged for forgiveness. I promised to change. But nothing seemed to work. I spent hours and hours reliving her dreams, trying to believe in them again. But she, and the dreams, kept slipping away. I studied her face in old pictures and thought about how beautiful she was. I closed my eyes and remembered feeling safe and secure in *her* skin. I felt afraid of being someone else. I had grown accustomed to *her* routine. She and I had wanted the same things before, had laughed at the same things before, believed in the same things before. And yet, like every sad love affair that comes to an end, she left because what *she* needed and what I could give *her* no longer fit, and the new "me" was left holding the shattered pieces of a broken heart that didn't even exist.

DaMaris B. Hill

Glory Days

Every morning she finds cracks and wrinkles in her reflection, tapping on the wall of mirrors that leads to the bathroom. She picks at them, the cracks, wrinkles and mirrors, frantically trying to separate the 1/8 inch of clear from the 1/100 inch of silver back and find the woman in between. She claws at the flat until it further weakens her nails into splinters. She knows that she is wasting. She walks away from the mirror for a third time this morning as she realizes the gunshots echoing in her ears are not strange voices of her imagination, but sounds from the 50-inch flat screen television that hovers near the roof of her room and watches over her as she sleeps. Its sounds combat her contentions about her bed and its isolation. She fears being alone. Gloria twirls sanity and success like twin pistols.

Ambivalent to the fact that she is sleek and invisible, like a bullet, she propels through life targeting situations and creating solutions where things were once impossible. No one has made a request she could not accommodate or problem she could not make solvent. She wants to save them from their fears, but she can't seem to get past their perceptions. Gloria spirals through a life she wishes wasn't so gray. She is twenty-something running away from her thirtieth birthday; life should mean something by now.

Gloria spends her nights in bars with slam artist superstars, starving artists and out of work actors – cons pimping poetry. It takes three glasses of wine for her to whisper to a stranger about her own writing that isn't shallow enough to pass for deep. She is bitter that she isn't drunk enough to promote self-pity and pain.

For Gloria life is like Russian roulette: pick a job, pick a social event and miss death, keeping it cool and sleek because no one expects her to spill. They freeze frame the shell casing before it kills them, ignorant to what's inside. She scribbles priceless poems on dirty cocktail napkins as he begs people to buy $15 CDs before she retreats to the safety of her loud TV and finally to the voices in her head. Every morning, she resurrects to save someone else, but gets distracted by a mirror, and the cries for freedom it carries from a woman she wants to know.

W. Clayton Scott

Colors of Hardware

Okay, you know how sometimes you walk from a room
in your house to another room, and when you get there you
forget why you came, so, you just stand there gazing distant
    like you've had a stroke or something.

Well, I walked into the room of today and couldn't figure out why I was
there. So, I walked back into the room of yesterday to hopefully jog my
memory (sometimes that helps). But suddenly I couldn't recall why
    I was in that room either.

As I stepped into an adjoining room, I saw my daddy standing alone. He
looked at me and asked me why he was there. And I said, "I'm just a little
boy; shouldn't you know since you're a Dad and all?" But he just walked
    through a door that led outside

and somehow he forgot his way back into the house. My mother stood in the
room of windows knowing exactly why she was there, but by then it was too
late. It was then that I had the revelation that it wasn't about the room
    of where I'd been or about the room

of where I was. Nor was it about the passageways, the hallways
and corridors. Nor was it about the doors themselves or the windows
in the room; it was about the hardware, and I found myself taking pictures
    with shudder speed slow and film

speed fast of hinges, ornate and common—and door knobs, vintage glass
or modern brass. Close-ups of locks with key holes and chains and latches.
In that moment there was the memory of attending the births of my children
    with images not of the portal that received my seed

or the passage that provided new life. But the hardware—the two clamps
on the cord and the surgical scissors sharp to cut and the gauze to catch
the blood. I saw the reflection of my dad at the Minneapolis V.A. Hospital
    in a comatose state, incapable

of speaking and wondering why he was there. I tried to explain but there was no way he could understand. I stared out a paned and frosted window, lost on aimless snow flakes that rested on the concrete ledge.

And I studied the hardware around the room,

the tubes that exchanged fluids and machines that spoke in languages
that I couldn't comprehend and the steel needle in an old purple vein.
As the windows of his soul were closing and the door to another room
was opening much too soon,

I sat on a padded chair with no camera to take shots of the door knob that turns or the hinges that let the door swing open. But I knew—I knew quite clearly why I was in the room.

Sounds of Human Comfort

They came this morning
unannounced. Always they
come without warning. Quick,
piercing blasts that scream, shrieking
obnoxious round toned sounds

that pour themselves into
the atmosphere of quiet.
Where do they go today? Not here—
nothing is wrong here. With this
I am comforted. Sirens comfort me.

Rise and fall. Rise and fall.
Inner ear tightens, eyes twitch.
Closer they approach. Loud
and louder. Muscles wait without
moving. Breath bends sideways beside

the quickened pace of madness.
Shoes hold fast to split concrete.
What tragedy has come?
Move along—not this address.
I find consolation. Sirens console me.

Dogs down the street
howl from the pain.
Red lights flash. Yellow blurs
splash across my pale bones.
Watch them pass. Spinning auditory

mayhem grows distant and fades.
I want so badly to howl.
Whom do they attend?
Not me—I am well.
I am caressed. Sirens caress me.

Elements of Reconsideration

The density of mass,
raw and incorrigible in between
right and wrong—the pause
that makes you question
why you run when you
know you should stand.
Indecision limps

behind you as a slipping reminder
of what you should forget
but fail in knowing how.
So, you open your broken
umbrella, shake a fist at the cold gust
that violates your chest,
and you angle your body

with resolute displeasure.
"It's not so bad," you convince
yourself under a hot shower.
Change will hold you accountable,
but you don't change
because you don't want
or need the annoyance

of maintenance and its
constant drone of necessity.
You don't belong here, but you
know that escape is not
dressed properly for the ball.
"No one will notice," you mutter
while knowing full well

that you have learned
the skill of believing your own
lies, enjoying the squalor
that a congregation of shadows
implies. They moan and complain
in past tense yet brag
about white-collar endeavors

dripping from holes in the present.
"Hold me up," you appeal.
"My caring has crippled
the judgments that have seduced me."
They have abandoned
their own excuses to blame
the graves of ancestors,

the ones with words weathered
away by indifference and time.
So, you resign in a cushion-less
chair by the window, turn down
the radio to whispers
and watch the night crawl
into the landscape of your gaze.

Alex Stein

Desperate Characters

Seven Desperate Phone Calls

One might say that the desperate are exceedingly clarified. One could certainly say that the desperate are exceedingly reduced.

Two cases of desperation:

A woman, in love, is driven to distraction by the inconsistency of her beloved. In the end she must decide either to love him as he is, or go mad trying to make him the person that she believes he could be.

A man, at the end of his rope, makes seven desperate phone calls. Seven desperate voices return his call to him. The madness accumulates. Finally he must make the eighth call, the one he knew he had to make all along.

Desperate times call for desperate measures, some say. Others say the measures were there all along looking for a way out.

The desperate come from different walks of life. You see them in the grocery store if you are looking. They hide so well, sometimes, it seems, and sometimes it seems one had been looking at their desperation all along, but it just now registered. In the town of Hurley Burley, the desperate walk around carrying wilted roses; that way we know who they are, and they know we know.

Most desperation is a by-product of isolation. But desperation breeds desperation until finally the isolation by which it was created is the least of its problems.

Another case of desperation:

Having no alternative he flew into a rage. Having no alternative, they put him in a cage. Having no alternative, he paced and turned inward. Having no alternative, he set about to erase the creature he had become, in the one place that would never allow him to forget himself.

We become desperate, probably, in most cases, trying to live up to the expectations of others. We become desperate children when we don't know what it is our parents want of us, much less why we were born. We become desperate adults when crisis precipitates our desperation. We become mature when we understand that crisis is a choice we make in the domain of will and perception.

They say the parrot in the cage wants desperately to fly free. But doesn't the parrot in the cage already have the whole universe? Some say the writer has freedom, but all the writer really has is an alphabet.

We become desperate when we feel to be fixed in an unsatisfactory system with no means of extrication. Calculate the number of systems that possibility allows and you will have calculated how many kinds of desperation there are.

Let us ask ourselves, what is the nature of desperation? It is a sense of unbearable lack. Lack of love, lack of community, lack of direction. Desperation is a grappling hook plumbed to emptiness.

What does desperation need? Hope. From whence does hope come? From the breath. By the vehicle of the breath.

Desperate Lives

In the early nineties, desperate to make a name for himself and to gain some acclaim for his art a young fellow named Knockson stood atop a bridge and proclaimed his allegiance to life. You see, he said, later, I had to do it in the posture of a suicide. Later, several young fellows stood where Knockson had stood. All of them jumped and perished.

Knockson: I did not want anyone to die from my affirmation. One cannot know every end that art will come to. Reporter: Are you desperate? At the end of your rope? How will you carry on making art? Knockson: I suppose as I always have. We shall see. I am desperate and I am sorry, yes, what will come of that, we will see.

Was Kafka desperate? That most dispassionate of self-observers. How would that desperation be measured? On what known instrument would it even register? To measure Kafka for desperation would be like measuring building blocks with spoons. Something wrong from the start. But let us say that if writing is an inducer of despair, we might estimate that writing like Kafka increases that despair about tenfold. But then what? Sharpens it. Buckles it on like a saber and bears it forward, to look at what it is, this world, and what he is in it.

Desperate Measures

The desperate will go back for their beatings, time and again, because they love the touch....for a moment, before the beating sinks in, the touch is all they know. Kiss, kiss, bang, bang, as someone else once said.

A soldier in the army of poets sat despondently at his table. An army of shadows marched before him. Each of those shadows promised to write his poems for him. Each one diligently, and he sat there, at his table, pondering.

I do not relish the spice of cruelty, says the one upon whom the desperate one has pinned all his desperate hopes, but in this case...weep until you have no more tears! That dread curse, in one of its manifold forms, is what has fallen on all the desperate. No, respite, no release. What is crueler than for an artist to die unnoted? For an artist to die unloved! But that far, even for the comic effect, is carrying the power that one person can have over another, too far. There is only so much giving over of oneself that is possible. Even the most desperate one of all cannot give over everything. Perhaps this is only because not everything belongs to him, but even so, it is the case.

Desperate to regain her love *He* abased himself. Desperate to redeem himself, *He* abased himself again. It went on like this. He getting farther and farther from himself. As out of breath as a landed fish. Desperate to regain her love, *He* even cut himself. That did it for her; she could not bear to be associated with this fiasco any longer. Solace was solace, but his was a case for Nurse Nightly and her team of white angels. A lost cause. A lunatic. Vincent Van What? Her friends tittered. Vincent Van Who?

We always fought, all the way along. We tried, both of us, very hard, to retire from fighting, but we both kept getting called back by the bells within ourselves. Fighting, fighting, all the way along fighting, and insisting all the while, in the love make-ups, that we had never had such strong responses to anyone, that something between us was being unearthed. That long slow painful process of discovery is what makes any relationship worthwhile, both the good ones and the bad.

Desperate Conversations

She: We fight over every little thing now. Didn't we used to love each other and promise to be gentle? You never did, you know. That's the only promise you ever made me and you never carried through on it. I suppose I have never known who you were all along. He: That's it. Let's talk it out. She: Nothing ever comes of our talking. Just more talking I suppose. More of your nonsense. Poetic suppositions. Half-baked ideas about our condition. He: That's your vision. She: No, that is us. He: No, that is your idea of what we are. She: Face the facts, fool, you are a train without an engineer and I am the only tracks you can run on. When I walk out that door it is not only goodbye to me it is goodbye to your last vestige of normalcy. He: I'll pull the brake. She: The brake? You? You don't know where the brake is.

He: I'll miss you. She: I'll miss you. He: You'll never be back, will you? She: You know we can't be together. He: I'll miss you. She: You'll get used to it. He: I'll never get over it. She: I didn't say that, I said you'll get used to it. He: There is a river flowing away, away, from inside of me, to dissipate in the most distant reaches of being. She: That shit, though, I won't miss at all.

He: If I could get a better job, would that change anything? She: It wouldn't change all the years I have waited. He: Oh, yeah, right.

He: I'd like to end this on a high note, if I could. She: Please, be my guest. If you think you can redeem all with a few more words, go right ahead. He: The desperate can make themselves free as easily as anyone else. No one, upon that point, should be afraid. One must simply awake to what is in the cup before one's eyes: the blessings of light. The blessing of what is.

A Brief Respite

What has anyone ever told you you couldn't do and you never afterward could do it? Who made you that decision? Or did your original face, the one you had before you were born, make it?

Kikaku writes: *Summer lightning!/ Yesterday in the East./ Today in the West.* This is the path of life. This traverse from East to West. Kikaku is the summer lightning. Yesterday in the East, today in the West. Death comes so quickly. That is the surprising thing. And takes with it so quickly everything that until then had only been dying.

You want answers? There are none. You want to be a bird, be a bird. That's your answer. There you go.

In the cave of the oracle there is a one-eyed prophet. That is all anyone can really tell you of their experience of reality. I will tell you one thing more, though: In the cave of the oracle, the one eyed prophet is king.

It is a curious sensation to pass through difficulties into ease. A boat untangled from reeds, now upon a smooth, fast river, it seems. But, this is just the heart, functioning as it should. That is all. It has never been anything other than that. It was nothing else in the tangled reeds beforehand, it is nothing else now.

And if there is no Great Confessor? If it is all just self-exhortation? Well, so what? Refuse to accept discouragement, someone once said and you are at the beginning of being able to grant your own Grace. Don't misunderstand me, I mean Grace the way Catholics mean it. And I mean 'at the beginning of being able to grant your own grace,' like the shaman means it, dancing under an ancient moon.

He1: I'm in love. He2: Great! He1: I'm in love with art. He2: Wait, let me get this straight. You called me over here to tell me you are in love with yourself? He1: With art. I'm in love with art. He2: Right. Yes. He1: You don't believe me? He2: No, no, obviously I do. He1: What, you don't think I believe myself? You think I am lying to myself? He2: I think you better know your history, is what I think. Has there ever been an art and it did not have to trick its way into existence? He1: Not an art that was worth the name. He2: Well, exactly.

In the moment when everything is untangling, the self becomes a masterful weaver. In the moment when everything is untangling, the self becomes a masterful weaver. There is almost nothing to which we will not tie ourselves when we see our worlds falling apart.

More Desperate Lives

Crazy artist turn out to be the norm, and no matter how long one resists it, the possibilities inherent in the system called art, which is really a system of reading signs, begin to overwhelm the mechanics of the mind that processes those possibilities. Take myself, for example. I started out normally enough. I could even have cited myself day by day as an example of what super-sanity might be. Nothing really bothered me for years. I was married. It was fabulous. I had children. They turned out fine. In my study, year after year, I was building a library out of my own head. Oh, the elaborations, the enumerations, the pumpkins and penumbras, the flaxen weaves of thought...But do you know what it was that broke me in an instant? The realization that all this had become my chains.

Literature is a labyrinth into which the author must enter. At the center of the labyrinth is the accomplishment of the author's every desire. But the author will not know the accomplishment is accomplished until the peace of it falls upon him. That is to say, with every next step the author might (but never does) find himself at that center.

Push up the hill the stone and you will learn what you are to that stone and what that stone is to you. Though this, unless Gods intervene (but isn't it usually just men and women doing it to themselves?) is your own choosing.

Tell a desperate one just to go and make himself happy. Go ahead, try and tell him. What is a desperate one desperate for if not happiness? Why wouldn't he just go ahead and do it? Because desperation narrows periphery until there is only a point. And a point, by definition, is that upon which one cannot come. A space, yes, one can come upon a space, even enter it, but a point, no, a point is entirely elusive.

The monster has his labyrinth, let him have it.

The schools have their learning, let them keep it.

Carl Gustav Jung. What a name. Jung's age, what an age. One in which a person of penetrating insight could rise and be noted. But what insight could penetrate the thickness of this age, our age? What insight could penetrate the fog by which one person and another seem to be separated? A fog of self-regard, it can only be called. One of the manifestations of this fog is fear. Another is war.

To take the measure of one's time, one must have the help of one's ancestors. Call them predecessors, if you prefer. Draw the lineage on a piece of paper if you like. They are still ancestors. Those who came (or whom we were) before we were ourselves.

Nothing has changed since the beginning, and nothing is likely to change; the thoughts with which we were born are there with us to the end. It is only our freedom that changes. The way in which we bear these thoughts, and with these thoughts, ourselves.

Same gain freedom through the breath, others by ceasing to accept discouragement; a rare few, by the success of their endeavors, a rare few more by love, by luck, or by grand design. I suggest the refusing of discouragement. It is the most hands-on.

There is more to the transmission than the transmission; there is also the reception. Of the two, if the latter is not in operation, than none of it can matter. Cassandra, who was given the gift of prophecy and then cursed to be unintelligible, dwells intolerably in exile, while the world degrades itself with what it calls ideas.

That, you might say to a desperate one, washed up upon the shoals of life, was not your destiny. No matter that you wanted it. No matter that you tried to make it that. She was not the end of your desire. No matter that you wished she could be. No matter that you tried to make that of her.

Rikki Santer

Mother to Son

I can't take your tiny hand anymore as you blurt
across the berm of another black hole, rolled

cigarette behind your ear. I'm a flat cartoon, steamrolled
into the next frame, my tiara tarnished and tagged.

You rear up onto your heels to spar, to tar
and feather my rationale before it can stand

on its own two feet. This opera stutters on a loop,
insomnia sputters on cue, and when you fold it up

like a game board—you always play it like a gamer—
another fingernail moon slips out and floats downward

to wedge between the floor boards
with the bread crumbs and spiders.

Overleaf

for Justin (1993-2009)

Lush maple felled across a road's curve,
limbs and branches dumb against passage.
You awake to this dream's freeze-frame where
you had hobbled backwards, filaments damp

and webbed in your socks, your pockets, trolls
folds behind your ears. From your hospital bed,
the forest dinnery is dank, your memory of rest
too distant. And now this dead tree, aptly thick

for deification, your banner pacing tartan and tall.
So many worry and wheeze and wait for you, their fingers
too numb to turn the next page. Instead they harvest
then harvest light from your forgiving eyes, tessellated
finery for the chromosphere of hearts.

Mourning Sickness

The hummingbird feeder sways crusty
and dry: dead red orb. The long idea
of your father perches in your lap
while a lizard traces the morning.

You waited fifteen years to arrive here,
his house far from yours in a gated desert:
this sunny home full of color whose floor
boards now split and spit, scolding

a gaping ceiling hole, cancerous
and established. Yesterday a dust storm
stung your eyes during his funeral at high
noon, a bullet shell now in your pocket,

souvenir of the three-volley salute.
The ambivalence feels like nausea—
Last-minute plane fare and car rental
you couldn't afford—but duty

is your last antidote for love withheld
a lifetime. Your bags are packed,
his patio stages your morning theater:
moon hands off to sun, son now the father

his should have been. At your ear's lobe
a hummingbird startles you, darts
backwards, and then before you can re-focus,
moves on.

Casey Clabough

Show & Tell

"Tell them I am going to show them what they are." This from my mother while dropping me off at primary school.

She'd agreed to come to Parent Show and Tell Day but we had to report to the teacher what our visiting parent would be talking about. I leaned forward to hug her and she kissed me on the forehead. I always looked up at her, reluctant to go.

"Go on now," she'd say after a moment.

But once I was out of the car I'd always turn around and wave, as if the hug and the kiss hadn't been enough. She would smile a warm, slow smile and then shoo me on with a flick of her wrist.

I'd walk away slowly so long as I could feel her eyes on my back. But when I sensed them move and heard the car pull away, I would stop and walk back, watching as she pulled out onto the road in front of the school. Her car was very loud and rumbled like a faraway storm. Unless a teacher made me move, I would wait listening until it reached the place half a mile away where the speed changed from 25 to 55mph. Then I would hear the sudden burst of sound that came when Mama stomped the floor. She didn't know it, but that was her real daily goodbye to me.

"Go Mama!" I would say in my mind and wonder if she heard me.

Her car was an old Mercury Cougar she'd bought years ago, before she quit her job. It had a V8 engine, like the drink I liked.

"Its getting old, like me," she'd say sometimes, "but its still got plenty of power. More than three hundred horses worth."

* * * * *

After lunch, the teacher went around the room, having inquired of the class who had a parent coming and what they would be showing or telling.

"My mom's a secretary," said the girl sitting next to me. "She's going to show how fast she can type and then give us our words to take home."

Then it was my turn. "My mom is going to show you what you are."

The teacher, frowning. "What does that mean?"

"I don't know. It's what she told me to say."

Class snickering, slow blush filling my face.

Teacher again. "What does your mother do?"

"She can do a lot of things, but she almost always stays at home."

60

"So your mother is a homemaker."

"Maybe. I don't know what that word means. I've never heard it before."

Low sing-song whispers from a corner of the room. "Housewife, housewife."

"Shhhh! Shhhh!" said the teacher, growing irritated. Then to me, "There's nothing wrong with being a homemaker, but you should ask your mother if there is anything special about what she does before she shows and tells. A lot of what homemakers do is unremarkable and the same. We don't want all the visiting mothers to say the same things."

*

I cried sometimes during naptime because I missed Mama so much. To help with this she had given me a toy version of her car that was exactly like it in every way. I would lie on my mat and run the car over my chest and up and down my arms making a soft low sound like faraway thunder.

But then in my mind I could see her face at home and tell she was unhappy. My head began to throb and I would cry, softly and quietly, hot tears running over my temples and curving round my ears. It hurt my heart to know she was all by herself and unhappy. I wished I could be there with her. When the teacher grew angry and told me to stop crying, I always felt bad and apologized.

I wanted to stop crying, but I couldn't.

*

By the time my mother completed her doctorate at the Medical College of Virginia in the late 1960s, her research had made her one of the world's experts on the pineal gland, and so she received the rare professional privilege of a job offer from the school that had granted her terminal degree. She had been the only woman in her graduating class and, when she accepted the job, the only woman faculty member.

The first course she ever taught was in a large, sloping, concrete-floored lecture hall. One entered at the back and made a long descent to the stage, where stood two long chalkboards and a lab table.

Mama nearly always ran late so that on the first day of class, when she entered the auditorium at the rear, arms full of books and lecture notes, the students, over a hundred of them, all men, were assembled and waiting for her. Her lab coat distinguished her as a professor, but the expressions on their faces as they turned to consider her—disappointment, anxiety, dismissal—told the tale of their collective shock.

Whispers as she begins the slow descent to the stage, heels clicking steadily on the concrete. About halfway down someone launches a brief, piercing whistle—ancient trumpet sound of male admiration—applauded by sporadic laughs from his fellows.

Mama keeps walking.

At the bottom she mounts the two steps to the stage and walks to the lab table, where she sets down her books before looking up around the lecture hall, squinting slightly in the lights, taking in the vague sea of male faces.

She takes off her coat.

"That's right! Take it off!" cries an anonymous voice somewhere off to the left.

"Take it all off!" exclaims another on the opposite side of the room.

Burst of laughter from all sides.

Hands trembling slightly, Mama takes hold of her lecture notes and turns to write on one of the chalkboards.

"Nice ass!" a voice calls.

Then a hollow, slightly grating sound of motion and muffled laughter. Turning from the board Mama spies an empty jar rolling down the central aisle, students seated to the far sides of the auditorium half-rising from their seats so as to follow it with their heads. Picking up speed, the jar hits against the bottom stage step and careens to one side. More muffled laughter.

Mama turns back to the board and keeps writing, listing her key terms for the day.

A minute passes, etched sound of idea transformed into symbol.

Then, again, the rolling sound—closer, louder, varied in texture—as the jar rolls over the boards of the lecture stage. Mama turning just as it glances off her shoe. Loud laughter this time.

As the sound dies, Mama walks to the lab table and sets her chalk down. Then she takes off her glasses and sets them down too. As she looks back up and out over the indistinct audience a slow, warm smile forms on her face—the easy natural smile of a cheerleader or prom court princess, both of which she had been. She looks to one side of the auditorium and then to the other, hands on hips, smiling.

"Cutie!" calls a voice.

"Hottie!" says another.

Smile still intact, unwavering, Mama strides across the stage to where the jar lies resting. Hands still on hips, attitude of sensual affectation, she lifts her right foot, arches an eyebrow at her audience, then brings it down suddenly, heavily, air of the room pierced as glass shatters, echoes, jagged irregular pieces sliding across the stage in various directions.

Silence, pause, then the lonely sound of Mama's heels as she walks back to the table, puts on her glasses, and looks up around the lecture hall.

"Let's get to work, gentlemen."

* * * * *

"There is . . . a class of monsters who might live, but which would always remain freaks."
—*Charles Sumner Bacon, "A Symposium on Obstetrical Abnormalities" (1916)*

Sitting on a shelf in a little windowless supply room just off one of the dissection labs was the Medical College's collection of genetic mutations: a dozen infants and fetuses afloat in large, clear glass containers of formaldehyde. I used to dream about them when I was younger.

The variations of these beings were obvious and subtle, shocking and secretive. Several were possessed of different degrees of encephaloceles, the meninges protruding from their heads' occipital region in a number of different shapes and geometric designs. What would that feel like? One was visited with holoprosencephaly, its nostril displaced and its optical qualities all fused together into a great single orb. What might such an eye have seen? And an instance of doubling to balance this cyclopean collapse: an infant possessed of one body and two heads, the result of duplication of the neural tube. What would these heads have said to each other? What would they have thought?

Later, in college, reading on my own, I would come across a poem about a baby that was half-child, half-lamb. "In a museum in Atlanta," it reads, "Way back in a corner somewhere/There's this thing that's only half/Sheep like a woolly baby/Pickled in alcohol . . . ." I thought so much of the poem that I resolved to study writing under the man who had created it, hoping perhaps to develop the powers to commit my own real and imagined monsters to paper—to afford them a kind of immortality through my rendering, which might also, in turn—I hoped—provide me with something at last from them. "Are we," asks my old literary master, "Because we remember, remembered/In the terrible dust of museums?"

When I dreamed of them, they would move, but they never left their containers. Their meninges would pulsate, throb, with life. The mouths of the two heads would take turns opening and closing, bubbles emerging into the vat's closed liquid world, traveling upward. And then, very, very slowly, as if awakening even as I slept, the lid of the great single eye would draw back and the enormous orb would regard me—neither warmly nor coldly—but with some vague aspect of feeling—watching.

Little lamb, who made thee?

Dost thou know who made thee?

I suppose they did look monstrous and terrible, but I was never afraid of them. They were my friends.

If they could have smiled at me, they would have. And I would have smiled back.

*

Sitting together in a pasture meadow, patched quilt spread out beneath us, Mama's arm resting across my shoulders. Afternoon sun of spring casting long shadows of tree branches upon the ground, where the breeze flutters slightly the new blades of grass.

A blue bird, landing less than a foot from my foot, chirping and turning its tiny head sideways to regard me. Then he hops—three short, plump, quick hops—to the end of my shoe and bends forward, craning his neck to examine it.

I whisper something and he searches my face before hopping onto my shoe, glancing at me again, then launching himself, soaring up and then back behind us, toward the trees that cast shadows.

I turn back from the bird's path to discover Mama watching me intently.

"Why did the bird come so close, Mama?"

"Animals can tell things about other creatures."

"You mean just by looking?"

"More than just looking. We can't really explain what they do because we are not them."

"The little bird could tell about me?"

"That's right. He could tell about you. That's why he came so close."

I lean my head against her and as I do she draws back her arm and then lets it fall, trailing her forefinger down my back, tapping each ridge of my spine as if marking a paper. Then the hand comes back up, fingers absently playing about my hair like butterflies.

"You are very nearly perfect," she says. "Just how I imagined you would be."

She draws me to her. "My precious creation."

After a while I pull away and look up at her. "Mama, I can tell about you. You're sad."

"I'm not sad, honey. I was only thinking."

"Does thinking make you sad?"

Short laugh. "It can, I suppose, but I'm not sad. You're here with me and when we're together I can never be sad."

* * * * *

She kept the skeleton in a corner of the upstairs cedar closet. It was easy to miss on account of all the various things clinging to different parts of it: winter caps stacked upon its smooth head, heavy old shirts and frayed coats flung over its shoulders, an assortment of Christmas ornaments hanging from its lower ribs, and a child-sized basketball resting in its pelvis. The piled hats leaned slightly to one side, affording the skull a jaunty aspect, while the rough clothing drooping from the shoulders hung irregularly. The basketball resting in the midsection suggested an impossible pregnancy, and the bone-suspended ornaments could not help but appear festive, speaking, it seemed to me, of some secret grisly truth yet to be celebrated. A big steel rod rose out of a metal base resting on rollers and ran upward through the spinal column before terminating in the skull, creating the illusion of a body somehow hovering in air of its volition, feet dangling three or four inches above the floor.

Despite the novelty of its presence, the skeleton really was just another item in storage—something put away, half-forgotten. Sometimes when I was helping Mama in the closet, she would address the occupant with "And how are we today, my good man?" or "Excuse us, sir" or "Don't mind us, old friend." She always seemed happy to see him—an acquaintance from another time; a fondly remembered ally from a war long over.

I would visit him sometimes when I was upstairs alone, getting a rush of cedar as I swung forth the door and flipped on the light. Carefully I would place my little hand against his, studying the contrast, and then pressing each of my fingers against a corresponding fleshless digit.

Even at that age I did not need my mother to tell me this was what I would be some day. That it was what lay in store. Some fundamental cognition knew. And it was comforting in a way, a privilege, to have this visual testament available day or night, close at hand and always the same, which seemed to say, "Beneath all the motion and coating of life, here is what you are."

I have no recollection of the truth of this ever troubling me. Perhaps it had something to do with the fact he did not seem to mind it so much himself. Whenever I opened the door, his expression was the same. He was always smiling.

* * * * *

65

Parent Show and Tell Day and Mama running even later than usual, the time for heading to school coming and going with her propped against her pillows, briskly flipping pages while sipping at her coffee.

"I'll just take you when it gets to be time for my visit," she said when I checked on her. "We'll visit school together. Now go and get me another cup."

Lunchtime passed and I was out in front of the house feeding butterflies, tips of my fingers all sticky with sugar water, when finally I heard her calling me. I blew gently on my forefinger to dismiss my guest before turning to run around back of the house.

At first glance I didn't recognize the woman standing next to the car as Mama, the figure in the sleeveless white spring dress and black heels and sunglasses appearing more like someone out of one of the women's magazines I had seen in doctors' offices. I hesitated, gawking. But then she smiled and waved for me to come on, and I knew it was her.

"Let's go," she called. "We're late!"

Spray of rocks and scattering of panicked chickens as we plowed up the driveway, windows all the way down and Mama humming softly to herself a song I did not know, while behind us, on the back seat, a third passenger lay sprawled.

* * * * *

Sliding to a stop between two buses in the circular school parking lot, not far from the main entrance. Car doors open, front seats leaned forward, Mama motioning me to climb into the back.

Gesturing at the skeleton's base. "Help me lift him, son."

Me, curiously strong for a child my age, grasping him by the rollers and heaving upward and forward, slipping a bit as I step out onto the gravel, banging a femur against the door.

"Careful now," says Mama, her steady hands clenched about his collarbone.

Then, me, letting down the base and together—me pushing and Mama pulling—bringing him upright. He sways slightly before leveling out between us, blinding white of bone and flashing metal in the end-of-school-year sun.

We roll him slowly, haltingly, over the gravel lot toward the entrance, me pushing while bracing the backs of his legs, and Mama steadying him, arm about his waist in the attitude a nurse will adopt while guiding a frail elderly patient.

Through the heavy school doors to discover emptiness inside, an industrial fan, nearly as tall as our companion, the sole occupant, blowing at the far end of a dim forlorn hallway, caressing our damp foreheads with warm air. Rolling him down the corridor, shut crayoned doors of classrooms passing on either side, the going much easier on the polished smooth floor though a wheel squeaks slightly, piercing occasionally the droning refrain of mechanically pushed air.

As we turn a corner a janitor steps forth from his closet, then, noting us, retreats wide-eyed back into it, drawing the door shut before him, water bucket sloshing—lapsing into a motionless silhouette behind beveled glass.

Arriving at last at the door to my classroom, student roster hanging on it with stars of different colors attending each name. Only a few next to mine, all of a lesser hue.

Mama absorbing this data in a glance, then hand on my shoulder, gentle and firm, moving me out of the way. "Stand aside, son."

Door flung open, swinging inward, and in rolls the skeleton, Mama pushing him from behind, teacher and students frozen in their places, mouths rounded and agape, eyes nearly as large. The skeleton coming forward, passing between the main center rows of desks and up to the very head of the room. He stops before the teacher and Mama steps out from behind, appraising the woman with a frank stare, looking her up and down. The teacher had always seemed to me very big and very frightening, but next to Mama—so tall and pretty and smart in her heels and spring dress—she looked small and old and plain. I felt sorry for her. The teacher's throat moved and she shuddered suddenly—at Mama or the skeleton I couldn't tell which.

When Mama turned to address the class she rolled the skeleton about with her so that they turned together, gracefully, in unison, like dancers or skaters, the teacher falling back away from them, like a lesser actress abandoning the stage.

Then Mama began speaking to the students and as she did a strange glow came over her which I had never seen before. "I am sorry we are late today for show and tell," she says, "but real learning never runs on time and for us I hope you will make an exception."

Quick glance at the teacher, who nods uncertainly, before continuing. "I believe my son informed you that I would show you what you are." Heads swiveling briefly to where I stand at the back of the class.

"Well," she continues, "here you are. Here is what you all are beneath your clothes and your skin. Look at your arm. Look at your hand. Then think about that for a minute. Think about it."

Students extending their arms, holding out their palms before them.

"Your human skeleton, this thing inside you, is very strong and very hard, yet it is relatively light. I bet your mothers weigh you sometimes. We like to know how big you are getting. In a man like this one who weighed maybe 160 pounds the skeleton is only thirty pounds.

"And it is perfectly adapted for locomotion and manipulation," she goes on, lifting the skeleton's forearm so that its elbow joint flexes. "See?"

Widening eyes at this.

"Now, it is our spines that are responsible for our upright posture," she says, running her hand down the skeleton's back. "Because we stand upright, we are able to use our hands in order to manipulate our environment. We reach out and we change things."

As Mama points to each bone grouping in succession, naming each again, the students watch her finger, then look down at the corresponding places on their bodies.

Stunned silence, then a lethargic stirring as if awakening from the same powerful dream. The teacher, off to the side, rigid and frowning.

"Is it a boy or a girl?" a boy asks.

"He was a man," says Mama, "a very old man.

"Where did he come from?"

"Southeast Asia," replies Mama. "I can tell because of his bone structure and cranial development."

A girl. "Where is that?"

"On the other side of the world," says Mama.

Another girl asks, "How did he come all the way here?"

"Sometimes when people die their bodies get sent to scientists so they can be studied. That is what I used to be: a scientist, a *woman* scientist. I studied bodies so that I could learn about how to work on the ones that are alive and make them better."

Students staring at Mama in wonder, a pair of girls peering uncertainly across the aisle at each other, suddenly possessed of new eyes.

"I like talking to you all," she says, smiling a warm, slow smile, and they all smile back at her. "Now for the real fun. Who wants to touch him?"

Eruption of hands and a piping chorus of "Me! Me! Me!" Bodies abandoning their desks, pressing forward as a body. My little classmates, weaving around the skeleton in a frenzy of fascination, quick touches from small forefingers—one girl reaching up to grab a bottom rib, then lifting her shirt to poke at her own.

And me, apart from the others, with eyes only for my mother: towering above the swirl of motion, commanding the classroom, beaming down upon the children, showing them themselves.

Kirby Wright

Black Butterfly

A black butterfly floats in through my open window, flutters around the bedroom. My god, it's as big as a bat. "No nectar here," I say. The butterfly joins a menagerie of bugs already sharing my walls: a pair of horse flies, a moth shaped like a funnel, and a beetle I'm certain is Japanese. I don't have a dog or a cat so it's nice having company. I will keep my window open and continue collecting; my only concern is that these bugs don't become institutionalized. I don't think they will because I don't feed them and don't pay their medical bills. They're free to come and go. It's nice having a family after your girlfriend leaves you for being a cheapskate, a snorer, and a claustrophobic. The butterfly lands on the panel covering the attic—it squeezes through a crack and disappears. Doubt I'll ever see that butterfly again. Maybe it will turn into a bat up there, live off ghost droppings and dreams that drift to the moon in the dead of night.

Bradley Earle Hoge

geometry of poetry

we die a geode our life the becoming how i love the splash of cold water on my face some sit and think while others sit and feel you must believe that memories exist separate from the mind like papers filed in folders when i'm ill i dream of geometry shapes falling tumbling cascading hoping to be beautiful hoping to leave large colorful crystals the cold earth in winter i am made from the cold ground and to some the rocks tell stories while for others they radiate meaning magnetic bubbles held in stasis immutable once created down upon me and i have to corral them like catching multidimensional rain from our slow formation our hardening molecule by molecule the ice man the arctic hare the turtle under Atlas' feet oyster's nacre surviving lustrous while roots break rock to soil and winds blow soil into oceans is that why you remember the color of my shirt and my words but not my tone gather each polymorphous rhomboid in my arms more than i can hold directed by precedent into historical structure through time succulent time and oceans rage and whimper as the earth waxes and wanes not the context of history words cannot be taken back should life be any different align the numbers representing sides with just enough imperfection to sparkle minerals replacing bone earth consuming life and oceans are lifted into mountains but emotion which has changed like memories as synapses break and reform but I can never accomplish it they bounce out of reach or fade from my grasp vague in location in space and time just enough impurity for color consummated by destruction i am the unconformity that proves existence which crumble and the molecules of your body are replaced each and each while somehow the pattern is maintained as i search for them again and again i am always alone in this dream assigned my task i cannot wake until it is accomplished for it is only in dying that we become solid eternal the splash of cold water against cliff face carving my name into the earth and some sit and dream while others sit and wile away the hours somehow the words still hang in the air shapes put in order everything taken care of impossible dream like all poets i write from this desperation

Janine Lehane

Diorama

The verandah is crested
with hanging plants: coleus
lavishly spinning a tale

for the glossy bromeliads,
laid at excellent intervals
on the planks that bear

baskets of macadamia nuts,
anodized milk tins,
a smart wireless radio,

and Grandad's red chair.
Inside, linoleum,
cool as you please,

the miracle of fruit flies
at the over-ripe mangoes,

Grandma's green chair -
for her back - with springs
and cushioning,

the Yardley talcum powder
and lady's perspiration
and resting in one's slip

on the green chenille
bedspread and Humpty,
forever surprised

according to
the Simplicity
pattern.

This is the rice
paper I walked,

tracing lines
accentuating, adjusting,

the bite of scissors
through cloth

and picking up
chores to aid
creative production

my feet on woolen
carpeting, elegant grey
with pink roses.

We all knew anticipation
and the dread
of interrupting

a dress, a cloak
a beautiful piece
and spinning

to show you
this new evidence:
this is joy

in pleats and tucks
and frills
and stitches

and lines
and joins
and drapes

and god-knows
how we'll get
it done in time,

flowing
and bunching
over polished wood,

miles of fabric
run across
the polished wood.

Diane Hoover Bechtler

Armed

1. I still smell the earth and hear birds and see the sun blaze.
2. But, I miss brushing my own teeth, cutting my steak, grabbing a hamburger or a French fry.
3. I long to fluff my cat and puck a ripe peach, plant a flower, water a flower.
4. At dinner, I see silver forks not lifted and crystal wine glasses in sunbeams where they create rainbows.
5. The nails on my limp hands hanging off immobile arms are painted red,
6. Most of all, I miss holding the grandchild I do not yet have.

Deborah L. J. Mackinnon

Cat Scratches

The leather couch lulls her to sleep more often than her bed where her husband snores into her right ear. The smell of the leather sedates her along with the angle of the cushions and that fact the living room offers her solitude. Still, she sleeps with one ear peeled for the front door left ajar, a flashback to late night teenagers. Her mother did this, slept on the couch waiting up for five children. She only did it for three. So, is she following a parental pattern of also distancing herself from an aging spouse?

Together they picked this condo, bought new furniture and moved the cat to town. Felix, a sleek black male, has become the "child" in their relationship only they've reversed roles. Now, her husband is the nurturer and she's the breadwinner and disciplinarian. They take turns getting up for the cat. Felix has already been out twice this night. Deep sleep is impossible while she listens for his scratching on the screen door. Would it be so horrible if she didn't hear him?

Theirs is a second marriage for each of them. Only now, after twenty-two years and three grown children, are they childless except for Felix. Decades ago their nine years age difference hardly mattered. Now, some days it multiplies exponentially. He's preceded her into retirement, beta-blockers, and relegated exercise; and vindictively predicts, "Just you wait!"

Their children have yet to embrace the new place. They still grieve the sale of their childhood home. The eldest once complained, "You have to understand, we grieve for the only home we've ever known and just want our mommy to tell us it's going to be alright." She, in menopausal fervor, retorted, "And I just want my adult children to be happy for us and to tell me it's going to be alright."

All three adult children blamed her when the cat ran away. The first time, clothes left at the front door directed Felix back to the new condo after two days. The second time, she alone believed he was still alive after two weeks. Her children put all their grief into their pet. Felix's absence symbolized their loss. And, her husband pragmatically refereed.

Unexpectedly, an early morning phone call brought news of a Felix sighting and retrieving the cat played out like a Hallmark commercial in slow motion. His subsequent acceptance of the condo prompted acceptance all around making Felix the crown prince of the domain. The stability of the couple's lives seems inexplicably tied up with their cat. Maybe they need the anchor.

The night, the solitude, and her reflections on aging are companions to her watchfulness. Upon hearing scratching, she gets up. But her spouse is already cajoling Felix back indoors. Undetected, she returns to the couch smiling at her husband's gentleness. Synchronized with his turning of the dead bolt lock, she plops down on the leather cushions and falls fast asleep.

J.D. Blair

Doc Su

Doc Su's lattice sheltered home was awash in the perfume of lilac and herb, pungent, serious scents that washed over you as you entered his house that served as his office and treatment center. Su was a Chinese herbalist treating my father who at the time was a policeman in our small town located in the San Joaquin Valley, the sink of the great basin of California. I often accompanied my father on his visits to see Doc Su who ministered to my father's throbbing kidney. As a young man he lost one kidney to tuberculosis and Doc Su was helping him deal with the pain that was attacking the remaining kidney that eventually failed and caused his death at forty-nine.

At some point early on in his role of public protector my father did a favor of some kind for Doc Su and his two daughters and in return for the favor the doctor more or less adopted our family and was forever repaying whatever kindness my father had shown him. On more than one occasion, out of the blue he would call my mother or father and ask, "Do you want Chinese food?" The answer of course was always yes. The good doctor and his daughters would bring to our home all the ingredients and utensils he needed to perform his culinary magic and would commandeer my mother's kitchen. I remember him telling her, "You sit, I cook." And cook he did. The house soon filled with the aromas of fried egg rolls, won ton and mushroom soup. Mounds of chow mien steamed in large pots; the sizzle of sesame and pork and beef vegetable stir-fry crackled throughout the house.

After cooking a meal for five that dear man would serve it to our family but he never ate with us. He sat and chatted with us for the entire time that we ate. Afterward he and the girls would clean the kitchen, take his pots and pans and leave, refusing any sort of monetary payment. Kindness in payment for kindness.

Regina Murray Brault

1947 Family Portrait

Daddy was in a gang of gandy dancers pounding nails
to hold the rails in place. By sundown, his skin hung
coal-soot black, and bent. Mama worked inside a
factory inspecting faulty fingers of the woolen
gloves. Her weapon was a silver needle that poked the

wayward strands back into place. My job was dirty, just like
Daddy's. I carried buckets to and from a neighbor's coop and
buried weekend guts and decapitated heads. My place was
caretaker of bull-fish heads and chicken droppings, and veggie
garden weeding; all honorable tasks that helped us fill our plates.

Debra Baker

Losing Shawn, Losing Me

A huge, round overhead light blinds me. Masked people covered with green hospital gowns, hair hidden under caps, bustle around, talking to each other while doing their jobs. I lay on a table, numb from the waist down, a relief from the searing pain I felt five minutes ago. The drugs numb my fear, as well, but I wonder how my legs stay in the stirrups. The room is cold and I turn my head from side to side, anxious to see what happens next. A faint smell of disinfectant mixes with the odor of the hospital.

The walls are painted a lighter shade of green, strangely soothing. A nurse gives me another shot in my IV, a doctor pulls the overhead light down close to me, and the next time I open my eyes, I see an ugly mass emerging from my body, the doctors looking intently between my legs. "Ok, placenta is out." I fade out briefly as they clean me up, but hear one of the doctors say, "You have a boy," smiling, and a nurse brings a bundle to me.

I feel disappointed at not seeing the actual birth of my son, but it's over. The nurse places the tiny, warm body in the crook of my right arm. He is wrapped, papoose-style in a lightweight blanket. I look at his little scrunched-up face, pink skin, and dark hair peeking out from his blanket. How will I give him up? I don't want to think about that right now.

* * * * *

Whenever I hear the words "unwed mother" or "illegitimate baby" the titillation is palpable. They are whispered words, shameful words. Of course, the only girls that these words apply to are the "loose girls," the "easy girls," the "bad girls." When a girl "got in trouble," everyone knew what that meant. Who could fathom any of this in 1967, in the small town of Walnut Creek, California, where the big event of the year is the Walnut Festival?

But here I am, eighteen, just out of high school, single and pregnant, "in trouble." I need to find a "maternity home," also called a "home for unwed mothers," where I will go to hide until my baby is born. Then I will relinquish him for adoption. Three of these homes exist in the Bay Area, and it is my job to go to each and see how I like it, if that is even a possibility. Being forced to live in a strange place amidst strangers doesn't seem like something anyone would like to do.

Before finding a home, I meet with an adoption caseworker, Mrs. Moore, part of Social Services in Contra Costa County, where I will sign the adoption papers. My mom comes with me, and the two of them figure everything out. That meeting is pretty much a blur.

September 6, 1967 Intake Notes: Deborah Baker

Client of average height, dressed in a full-sleeved blouse and skirt. Her hair is in typical "hippie fashion" and she wears only heavy eye make-up. She is exotic looking, and appears relaxed and poised. She prefers to be called Debbie instead of Deborah. She is accompanied by her mother, and they just came from a medical appointment where having an abortion was discussed.

"So, Debbie, what are your feelings regarding the baby?" the Mrs. Moore asks.

"I wish I could have an abortion, but the doctor said I am too far along."

"And now you are considering your options about the baby? Are you considering a maternity home?"

"Yes, or maybe staying home and hiding being pregnant."

"That won't work, Deb," my mom interrupts. "How are we going to keep you hidden for the next five months?"

"Are you considering adoption to please your family, Debbie?"

"I'm really mixed up, nothing is the right decision."

September 19, 1967 Notes: As Debbie's doctors would not recommend an abortion, she will be placed in a maternity home, once she decides which one is acceptable for her. She seems to have a good deal of feeling about the baby, while making it clear that she would rather abort it.

My mom and I drive around Oakland, looking for the Salvation Army Booth Memorial Home. I took a wrong turn and we find ourselves in a rough area. I take another turn, right in to an anti-war demonstration. Young men and women march in the street, holding "Stop the War" signs, yelling "Hell no we won't go!" and there are lots of cops. It's a noisy scene, one that threatens to turn bad at any given moment, and we don't even get out of the car. I catch a glimpse of an old brown shingle building, standing forlornly in the middle of the block.

As I drive to San Francisco for an appointment at St. Elizabeth's Infant Home, located at the top of Masonic at Geary, I wonder how my life would be right now if I wasn't pregnant. If I drive all the way down Masonic I will hit Haight Street, my hangout the last months of high school, before I got pregnant, when things weren't so complicated. The home, a massive red brick structure, surrounded by a wrought iron fence, is hard to miss. The facility is well maintained and the older woman who greets me seems nice. The home has its own hospital, where young women labor alone, and deliver their babies into the cold hands of the nuns. But girls are not allowed to see or hold their babies, and I think that is cruel, so I know I am not going to live there.

On this early October day the air is warm and the soft breeze carries the smell of dried leaves. The drive to San Francisco takes less than an hour. I love going over the Bay Bridge, the vast green water of San Francisco Bay shimmering as far as I can see. Driving through the tunnel on Treasure Island feels like the halfway point to a whole new world, which it is. It is the world of the Haight, and the Fillmore, free concerts in the Panhandle, and wild, colorful clothes. I wear my navy empire-waist mini-dress with the big Kelly green polka dots. It is the style of the day, but given the mild temperature, the long sleeves make it a little too hot.

Exiting the freeway, I head to Broderick Street. No landscaping breaks up the stark grey of the sidewalks, and pieces of trash float in the air. The street is empty of life. I see the brick building with Florence Crittenton on the façade, and look for a parking space on the street. As I approach the entrance, all I can think of is this will be my new home for the next five months. I just need to remain composed during the interview. The big door slams behind me as I enter the building, and I think the noise must be what a cell door in prison sounds like. I stand in a large reception room with small divided areas and a woman behind each glass window. A kind looking woman motions me over and I take a seat on the hard chair across from her.

The Florence Crittenton Home for Unwed Mothers is my last "choice." It has to be okay. The woman from behind the glass in the lobby shows me around. Shared bedrooms and bathrooms are upstairs, off-limits to visitors. A large communal dining room and living area occupy the downstairs. Young women in various stages of pregnancy, some talking together, some knitting, some playing cards, are seated around the living area, and it doesn't seem so horrible. I note (with surprise), that they all look normal, like me. I think it's really weird that I am instructed, like all of the girls at "the home," not to tell any of the other girls my last name.

October 4, 1967 Notes: Debbie was quite distraught, and explained that she took LSD and was afraid the baby might be born deformed. She expresses the thought that maybe the baby would be born dead. Tears rolled down her face as she contemplated her options. After she calmed down she concluded, "There is no right decision about my baby. If I keep the baby I cannot give it a good home, support it, or anything. If I give the baby up, the baby, when he grows up, will probably wonder why I didn't keep him and hate me for giving him up."

As a condition of being connected with Florence Crittenton, I am required to attend weekly counseling sessions with a social worker, so I walk next door to meet her. I make my way up the dozen steps of the light green Victorian, and enter the building announcing myself to a young woman at the reception desk. "Just have a seat. Mrs. Bartley will be with you in a minute." I notice the long hall with offices off to either side. An attractive brunette exits an office, walks towards me and introduces herself.

"Deborah?"

"Yes."

"I'm Mrs. Bartley." She offers a smile. "Let's go to my office." Her manner is warm and I immediately take a liking to her. "I understand you will be living at Florence Crittenton and will be signing adoption papers after the baby is born?"

"Yes, that's right."

"Well, we will be meeting every week to talk about how you are doing and feeling, and whatever concerns you have."

"That sounds like a good idea. I am really confused."

She suggests that since I am eighteen, I could live in an apartment, which is not far from Florence Crittenton. Four of us would live in a two-bedroom unit, with four more girls upstairs in another unit, but still under the auspices of the home, where we could take classes and go twice a week for dinner. I like this "option" better. She gives me the address of the apartment and sends me over to take a look and meet my new roommates.

She will give them a call so they can expect me shortly.

Driving back to Walnut Creek, aware of the afternoon heat beating through the windows of my dad's white Plymouth, I wonder what will happen to me. I don't want to think about any of it, so I turn up the radio and drown out my thoughts with Grace Slick singing "Somebody to Love."

At dinner, describing my day, I feel like I am describing a college dormitory in anticipation of going off to college. This is the first time I leave home and I'll be living with young women I don't even know. But it isn't the excitement of college; it's an imposed sentence. I think my mom is just happy that I'll be gone; she won't need to worry about someone showing up and finding out our secret. As I am in no position to bargain, I take my penance. I will leave home, have the baby, give my baby to strangers, and return as if nothing ever happened.

October 18, 1967 Notes: Another pregnancy in the family has apparently impacted how Debbie's parents relate to her, or at least that is her perception. She feels that her mother has bent over backwards to teach Debbie what is right and insisted that her way was right. Debbie feels that "everyone has to make their own choices as to what is right." She feels she has to decide for herself and then not care what people think.

My parents drive me to the apartment. We maintain a thick silence. I feel like crying but am resigned. My dad pulls up to the green stucco building, the white trim peeling, one of many houses and apartments lining the street. A little store sits on the corner of Masonic and Fulton, and some trees break the starkness. Knocking on the door, a young pregnant woman opens it and introduces herself. Curly strawberry blonde hair frames her face. We follow her up the indoor staircase to the flat. My parents don't stay long, just long enough to meet my roommates. I only have two maternity dresses, a nightgown and some underwear, so unpacking will be easy. I didn't bring any pictures or mementos from home.

The bedroom I'll be sharing looks out on to Masonic Avenue, a busy boulevard. There is nothing striking about the décor; just kind of drab and a bit shabby. Two twin beds wait for someone to lie down. The small bathroom has a shower, but no tub, and a window opens to an airshaft between apartment buildings, where the smell of old cooking swirls with trapped air. A tall window in a corner of the living room offers a view of the back staircase, and a worn couch and unmatched chair are placed on opposite walls. A television sits on a small wooden table next to the window. The kitchen, big by apartment standards, is furnished with a Formica table and chairs, and a window above the sink lets in a sliver of light.

I am in shock at being dropped off at a strange apartment, to live with women I don't know. The one thing we have in common is our pregnancies and the need to hide the obvious fact that we did something horrible. Nice girls didn't get pregnant, and in 1967, in the eyes of my mom and the world, that was the worst thing that could happen.

My three roommates are twenty-four to twenty-six years old, and because we will deliver at different times, my roommates will change over the next five months. I settle in as best as I can, and get to know them, first names only. They had already been out in the world, lived on their own, been to college, all of the things I wanted to do. And I am stuck in this apartment, away from home, not knowing what will happen, with nothing to do except wait.

November 1, 1967 Notes: She remains concerned about the baby being normal and is distressed to realize that the baby might not be as desirable because of her drug history and the lack of information about the father. She wept copiously.

My oldest roommate teaches me how to knit so I can make a blanket for my baby to have, to remember me, to know I love him or her. I buy a soft white yarn, with blue, pink, green, and yellow woven through. It takes a long time to knit, but it is a labor of love. When I complete the blanket, I run a pale green satin ribbon through the little openings placed around the entire blanket. The ribbon separates the blanket from a slightly ruffled hem. It is beautiful. I will wrap my baby up and never let him go.

The University of California Medical Center and the Women's Clinic provide maternity care to the girls at Florence Crittenton. Riding up Masonic Avenue to the hospital, the bus passes through the Haight, and I see the young people on the street. I feel so removed, like I will never be a kid again.

My mom blames the rock culture of the Haight for my situation. Surely, I was caught up in the counter culture, and did not have the experience or the means to take care of myself. I had no sex education at home or in school, and found out that the only "free love" was for the guys. Many young women like myself were getting caught up in that mantra and ending up pregnant.

November 29, 1967 Notes: Debbie has been giving some thought to the possibility of marrying the father to "give the baby a name" and then having the marriage annulled. She is embarrassed as she discussed her naiveté about birth control and her previous sexual relationships. She spoke to a counselor at school and opened up to the counselor in a way she could not do with her own mother.

I have a crush on my doctor, the chief resident in obstetrics. He is tall, has wavy dark hair and wears glasses. He is not that handsome, but he is kind and I never feel judged. I fantasize about being married to him and how he would take care of the baby and me. The nurses in the clinic are also supportive, and one in particular, a very tall blonde, a robust woman in her late twenties, teaches me how to walk so I don't have the pregnant waddle. "Stand up straight, tuck your rear end in, don't lean back," she instructs, and I practice diligently.

Sitting in Mrs. Barley's small office, we talk about my pregnancy and giving my baby up for adoption, as well as my keeping the baby and how difficult that would be. Single parents are not common at this time; the social structure does not support "unwed mothers" and their babies. As we talk, my mind drifts. Mrs. Barley is married with a young son. I wish I was her, able to see my baby grow up. I try to come to terms with a decision that I know isn't really mine to make.

My adoption caseworker is much older than my social worker and her job is adoptions. She tells me it is selfish to think of keeping my baby, that giving my baby up is the right thing to do. She reminds me every time I see her. But she is nice enough and I guess she want to make sure the adoption goes smoothly.

December 5, 1967 Notes: Debbie mentions her interest in meeting and possibly knowing the prospective adoptive parents. I explained to her that because agency adoptions are closed, this was not a possibility. Reluctantly, she accepted this reality but said she would spend some time thinking about the characteristics she felt would be important for a family to have.

The Old Spaghetti Factory in North Beach is a favorite and six of us pregnant girls are having dinner. The garlic and olive oil spaghetti is my favorite, and I wipe my chin, getting another bite of pasta. With salad and garlic bread, it's about $3.00 to stuff myself.

The restaurant is loud and the long communal tables invite others to sit, though no one does. Sitting at the table, our growing bellies aren't visible, so we could be a group of young women out having fun. I love the funky décor, and huge hanging lights, which give the place a little bordello charm.

Occasionally, we all get on the bus and go to the beach. I'm sure it is a strange sight, and I could have felt ashamed, except for the wedding band I wear so people think I am married. I wear the ring as I walk across the street to the big market to buy groceries for myself. We all make our own meals, and tonight I am making vegetables and swordfish, which is inexpensive. I live on a small check from Social Services, so I buy what is affordable. I told the butcher my husband is in Vietnam but I think he knows I'm lying. He is nice enough not to ask.

Sitting on the big brown, scratchy chair in the living room, watching TV while I eat my dinner, I can rest my plate on my belly, my own personal TV tray. The other girls think it's funny and we share a laugh. I'm eating late, and the girls go to bed. I stay up to watch Johnny Carson, munching the Hostess cupcakes I bought at the corner store, and washing them down with a glass of milk. This is my usual ritual, but some weekends my dad picks me up and takes me home for a couple of days.

I enjoy being in the car with my dad, riding across the Bay Bridge, east towards Walnut Creek. My dad is not a big talker, so there isn't much conversation. There is too much to say, and the difficulty trying to describe our feelings is overwhelming for both of us. My dad did tell me once that if I wanted to keep the baby, it was okay with him. But my mom has the stronger voice, and there would be no baby coming home with me. She felt my pregnancy reflected on her as a mother, that she failed to raise a "good" girl, and everyone would talk about us. My dad isn't concerned with what people think, but he is not able to stand up to my mother.

The lights on the bridge twinkle against the black sky. It almost seems normal, but everything changes when we get to town. We can't risk having anyone see me. That could lead to questions or people stopping by our house to visit. So I scoot down in the front seat until we get home and safely parked in the garage. Once in the house, with the drapes drawn, we can let our guard down somewhat. If anyone comes by, I hide in my room until they are gone. What did I think during those times? I feel that I deserve to be hidden, my shameful secret pushed in to a dark place where no one can find it.

December 6, 1967 Notes: Though Debbie has considered keeping her baby, she realizes she must give it up. She recognizes either way there is not a perfect solution, as she will always wonder about her child, but she is not ready to be a mother. Still, she feels she could be an adequate mother as she has love and affection to offer and feels she can fulfill the child's needs. She admits there is no financial support available and questions somewhat her ability to offer emotional security. She does not feel prepared to leave her parent's home and they are clear that she cannot bring the baby home. Debbie would like her baby to be raised in a family who could not have children of their own, who were not fanatical religiously, or excessively rigid or stifling. She hopes her baby will be raised to be himself.

As the months progressed, roommates came and went, the days stretched before me. Two nights a week, if the weather was agreeable, all of us walk over to Florence Crittenton to have dinner. Long tables are set up, and we visit with the girls who live there. There are no pretenses. All of us are there because we did something bad and our expanding bodies are the undeniable truth of our offences. But in that place, we can also relax, laugh and be ourselves. A young man works there, kind of like a den mother, and he is nice to everyone. It must be a strange job for a good-looking man in his twenties.

The classes offered at the home are strange, like sewing and make-up, but nothing to improve our minds or maybe point us towards some work. There was even a fashion show, which I modeled in. It was fun to go downtown to the maternity shop and pick out a dress to wear. It would have been nice to have another dress, but I had to give it back. I felt like I was playing charades, but after I had my baby, I was going to have to go back in the world as good marriageable material, and the classes would help us become good wives. And as long as no one knew my secret, I would still be able to find a nice man.

December 20, 1967 Notes: Debbie has been using her time "to get more perspective on her points of view." She sees herself as one who would do a lot of experimenting in life and try almost anything new. School has taken on a new importance and she hopes to "make something of herself and boost society." She feels she would not get further involved with LSD but I'm not sure she feels the same way about marijuana.

Standing at my bedroom window, looking out at the cars, I imagine what people are doing. It is winter, darkness comes early, and the flashing lights of the speeding cars remind me of the light shows at the Fillmore or Matrix. A well-known musician drives by, probably on his way to do a show at the Fillmore. Everyone is living their lives, and I am in a state of suspended animation. I cannot go forward with my life until this is over.

It's a rainy day so I stay inside the apartment, working on my baby's blanket, staring out the window at the back staircase. The rain pounds against the window, blurring the outside. That's how it feels, too. The outside world is a blur. I am not truly a part of it; my world exists within the confines of my pregnancy. But I love being pregnant, and I take care of myself so my baby will be healthy. I feel good about myself when my doctor says how well I am doing. I can feel my baby moving and kicking, a foot pushing under my ribs until I am sore. I do not want the middle of February to come when it will be over. I am afraid of what is going to happen.

It's Christmas time and I am home for the holiday. I love this time of year. When I was younger I made candles to sell so I would have money to buy presents. I baked cookies and decorated. The colored lights sparkle on the tree and I try not to think about my situation. I help my mom prepare tomorrow's Christmas dinner. I've been cooking and baking since I was a kid, and I make a marinated vegetable salad I wanted to try. I chop and mince and steam the vegetables, make a tangy dressing, and toss it all together to chill overnight.

My uncle and his partner arrive on Christmas day to celebrate with mom, dad, my sister, her husband, their baby, and me. But my uncle can't know I am pregnant, so when they ask where I am, mom tells them I am in bed, sick. They poke their head in the dark room and say a quick "hi." I mumble "Merry Christmas" and am glad the darkness hides my tears. I hear everyone enjoying Christmas, and when my mom pops her head in to see how I'm doing, the delicious turkey smell wafts in to my room.

January 17, 1968 Notes: Debbie appears open, conversational and intermittently introspective. She is very bright and she can succeed at almost anything she decides to do. A routine job will be too boring for her and the biggest problem regarding future employment will be finding a job that is stimulating enough. She expresses feelings easily and was moved to tears when she thought about the problems her baby might have in the future.

My mom and older sister come to visit today. My sister lives in Reno with her husband and baby and I haven't seen her since I've been pregnant. We haven't even spoken. My mom told her, and let her know what was happening about the adoption. I am happy to see her, and my little nephew. He is so big, crawling all around the apartment. We have a nice visit, but I can't stop thinking about how my nephew will only be eleven months older than my baby, and will never know his cousin.

Awakened from sleep at 6:00 am on February 28, the gnawing pain feels like menstrual cramps. I am two weeks overdue. I don't want to wake Marsha, my roommate, so I get up and find my way to the bathroom. My mouth is dry and I head to the kitchen, my bare feet chilled by the linoleum, reminding me it is February. I drink a little water and go back to bed. About an hour later, as the light permeates the window shades, I get out of bed, and standing, I feel a big gush. "Oh, no!" as the liquid runs down my legs, splashes my feet, and soaks the musty carpet. I can't move; a contraction has me in its grip. The distinct smell of amniotic fluid, the fishy smell of the sea, attacks my nostrils. My roommate wakes up.

"What's going on?"

"My water broke, and it really hurts."

"Ok, I'll get dressed and take you to the hospital. Can you lie down?"

"Maybe," not sure what to do, but knowing something started that I can't stop.

"I'll go get the car." Marsha is dressed in record time, amazing for someone eight months pregnant. "Take your time and meet me downstairs."

I make my way down the stairs, gripping the handrail, hoping another contraction doesn't come. Marsha pulls up to the door in her light blue VW bug. I heave my body in to the tiny seat, barely clearing the glove box. Marsha somehow fits her belly behind the steering wheel and drives me to the hospital, stopping in front of the emergency entrance.

"Wait here," as she gets out of the car. She enters the hospital and comes out accompanied by a nurse with a wheelchair. "I'll let everyone know. We'll come and visit," Marsha says, and she waves goodbye.

I didn't think about having anyone with me. This is something I will do alone, with help from the doctors and nurses, but there would be no husband, no mom, and no family support. I got in to this mess and I had to get out of it. Lying in bed in the labor room, alone and afraid, I don't know what to expect, but I know it is going to hurt. It is also the end of my pregnancy, and my future is uncertain. I became used to being in a cocoon with my baby, and that time is ending. I feel a profound sadness. I did not want to give my baby away.

Doctors and nurses come by to check on my progress. As time passes, the contractions become worse. I want the pain to go away. I do not want to be alone. My screams are primal, a reaction not only to the physical pain, but also to the reality of the inevitable loss of my baby. The anesthesiologist is finally called to administer the epidural, and after some time pushing, I am wheeled to the delivery room. Several ob/gyn residents, a chief resident, and some nurses prepare for my delivery. Everyone is nice and I am grateful for that. I want them to think I am a nice girl.

I name my baby boy Shawn Christian. Now that he is born, I do not want him out of my sight. I want him to stay in my room with me, but it is not allowed. I couldn't wait for the nurses to bring him to me so I could examine every little finger and toe, kiss his sweet face and breathe in his baby smell. I feed him his bottles and change his diapers, aware of each passing day bringing our separation closer. I tell him I don't want to leave him, searching his tiny face for some understanding. The residents and interns come to examine me, and I sense they do not know what to say. How can they? I'm not even on the obstetrics ward with the other mothers, as I'm not really a mother. I am giving my baby away, so different rules apply to me.

My parents visit one evening, but my mom seems nervous and they both seem uncomfortable. Though they bring a little gift for me, a tiny pink porcelain urn with a fake flower arrangement, there are no bouquets, no baby gifts. "Do you want to see the baby?"

"We stopped by the nursery on the way up to see you."

"Oh." I was surprised and disappointed. "Do you want to go see him with me?" My mom shakes her head "no." So there would be no proud grandparents walking with the mom so she could show off her new son. On some level I hoped that once they saw him, they would fall in love with this new grandson and want both of us to come home.

The day I leave the hospital, my sadness envelopes me like a shroud. I change out of my hospital gown, put on regular clothes and walk out of the hospital, leaving my baby boy and my shame behind me. Or that is what I am told will happen. The reality is that I leave the hospital with empty arms, and I know I will never forgive myself for letting this happen. Leaving through the big glass doors, I am numb. My roommate brings me back to the apartment, and then my dad picks me up to take me back home. At least I will not have to slouch down in the car when we get to Walnut Creek.

I gave birth only four days before, and my breasts ache for my baby. They will not stop leaking milk, and my mom binds sheets tightly around my chest to try to stop it. She takes very good care of me, bringing me breakfast in bed every morning. I do exercises to make sure I get my barely nineteen-year-old figure back so no one will be able to guess my secret. No one can know, and we never talk about the baby boy left in the hospital, waiting for the adoption worker to pick him up.

I worry about my son. He is all alone in the hospital, no mother, only the nurses. I was discharged on a Sunday, when no adoption workers were available. I begged to be allowed to stay one more night in the hospital, but was denied. When will he be picked up and taken to his foster home while awaiting adoption? Will he ever forgive me? Will he even know he has another mother somewhere? He will not know my identity because once he is adopted, the adoptive parent's names will be on a "new" birth certificate, and the original certificate will be placed in a closed file, the proof of something so bad it had to be locked away.

There are no classes that can prepare me for being a mother without her child. But I have no right to call myself a mother. I am single and my baby is "illegitimate," and that determines my ability to be a mother to my own baby. I could be married to a mass murderer, and I could keep my baby. I try desperately to decide what to do. But I know there is no way I can change my mother's mind. There will be no baby in the house, no proof of my badness, of my mother's failure. I am just putting off what is already decided, but I'm not sure I can live with the decision.

March 28, 1968 Notes: Debbie delivered four weeks ago and is here to talk about relinquishment or other possible plans for her son. She looks bad and appears to be really suffering and emotionally distressed. She acknowledges feeling miserable trying to think about what she can do for her baby. She wants him so badly and yet knows she has to give him up. Her ambivalence continues as she really is searching for ways to keep him, though she knows how hard it would be to raise a child out-of-wedlock. She is depressed, as she no longer enjoys her old friends. We spoke about the peace she might get from knowing that she had done the right thing for her son and having the strength to do it despite her own grief. She wants to see her baby again.

I go to see my son at the adoption office. They have a little nursery set up, and I have an hour to spend with him. I hold him and I tell him I love him and will never forget him. His tiny fingers clasp mine, as if to say, "Don't go." I bring his blanket, hoping the love I made it with will somehow reach him. I'm not sure I can leave him, but five weeks after leaving my baby in the hospital, I leave him again, at the Department of Social Services, with my adoption worker.

April 3, 1968 Notes: Debbie returns to spend time with her son. She spent every minute watching him and talking to him and could not believe how he had grown and that he was losing his front hair. She indicated she felt more at peace, although she was not sure why, as it was still going to be hard to give him up. She continues to feel depressed but insists that she wants to go ahead with the relinquishment, though she was still not sure how she was going to live with it. She had no question but that it is best for her son; that it's the only fair thing to do. Weeping, she pauses several times to gain her composure. Before signing the relinquishment she said she wants her son in a good home, and even more that that, she wants the family and her son to understand that she did not give him away but that she truly loved him. After signing the papers she cried quite a bit and finally pulled herself together and gave me the blanket she made for the baby.

Deni Ann Gereighty

Change of Life

It's a proper cookie sheet
although my life is not.
Twenty five years working
nights and evenings
four years of hospital stays
nursing home residence
and the rhythm of home health nurses
mark me indelibly.

At 1 AM I am awake
not even a pain cocktail
will sing me slumber.
Daylight hours are for sleeping
nights are for keeping vigil.

Babies to be birthed
kept me busy once.
Elder before my time
I keep watch for pain
ensure the sun will rise
take out the cookies
before they burn.

Moon

The radiant full moon startled me tonight.
Her shocking brilliance peeking through the evergreens
Nearly landed my car in a ditch.
This huge golden-white orb, luxuriant in her maturity,
Grows from nothing to an enormous size each cycle.
Taking all of her space without apology or embarrassment,
Unlike myself for most of my life.
My grandmother loved to tell the story of the night I was born.
The nurse delivered me during an eclipse of the full harvest moon,
Which the doctor was outside watching.
Tonight's moon reminded me of how I had lived eclipsed,
Bound by my fears and insecurities over my own size.
Drawn to my size positive sisters,
I hesitantly plunged into the glowing fire of self-acceptance.
Substantial, complete within myself, commanding attention,
I am growing into my fullest self.
Bountiful, taking ample space, I have learned,
I am beautiful as the Moon.

Number 1 Grandchild

Pepaw cracks open
pecans he collects from his trees,
tended carefully to avoid the blight
other local pecan trees suffer.
I eat his gift right from his hand.
Both of us ignore Grandma's call:
"A.J., don't spoil that child's supper."

He picks figs for me that I savor whole
until the skin irritates my tongue
so I suck the inner goodness
tossing stem and skin to the grass.

I gobble strawberries
as he picks them,
only if I am elsewhere do they
make it inside for grandma
to wash, cut, and sugar, and water,
cool them in the frig
until their own syrup develops;
a treasured desert.

Creole tomatoes he nurtures
go with dinner as long as I call
mom to be sure it is okay to eat with
my grandparents two doors down.

Come home from college for Christmas
he slips me a heavy present,
'Don't let the others see it, number 1'
I open the wrapping in secret,
my prize, a jar of his
pecan halves.

Lewis Gardner

Memory

We told my mother we wanted to do something special for her 90th birthday. She insisted we do nothing at all. She always discouraged us from making a bother over her.

After months of pressure, she consented to an Oneg Shabbat, or Sabbath celebration, in her honor, at the apartment building for senior citizens where she lived. Relatives and friends came to Revere, a town on the coast near Boston, from Connecticut, Maine, and upstate New York. Dozens of her neighbors attended.

When we were planning the event and told her that people would be asked to speak, there was a particular story she asked me to tell, and it was this:

Picture a restaurant and tavern in a seaport on the west coast of Africa. It's Monrovia, the capital of Liberia. The restaurant—small, just eight tables—with its bar, is exactly like something from a movie about the tropics. The bartender, Carla, a woman of mystery who never says exactly which European country she came from—or why—could be played by Yvonne DeCarlo.

The customers are from places like Vladivostok, Oslo, Beirut. I'm there because I'm in the Peace Corps. It's 1964 and I'm having dinner with a friend.

A plump, pleasant woman with a middle-European accent—she and her husband own the restaurant—comes over to our table and asks if I recognize the music on the p.a. system. I listen closely and to my great surprise, not only do I recognize the music, but it's an orchestral version of "Oyfn Pripitchik."

This never happens in old Hollywood movies.

I tell the owner, "Yes—it's something my mother sang to me." With a special smile—and yes, a twinkle in her eyes—the owner says, "I thought so."

In case your mother didn't sing it to you, "Oyfn Pripitchik" is about a teacher showing the letters of the Hebrew alphabet to little children. It's probably the best-known Yiddish folk song, although it may not actually be a folk song. The composer who popularized it in the 1800s either wrote the song himself or adapted it from a folk song he had heard.

I got to know the restaurant owner well. Everyone called her Mama Simonovich. She somehow survived World War Two in or around Vienna, along with her children. Her second husband—Papa Simonovich—had grown up in the court of the last Tsar of Russia. As a boy he sat on the knee of the Mad Monk himself—Rasputin—or Raspooteen as Papa Simonovich pronounced it.

According to Papa Simonovich, Rasputin intervened with the Tsar to help the Jewish population at the time of the pogroms, which was news to me. Papa's father published a book about Rasputin, in French, expounding the theory. I never read the book, although Papa showed me a copy, printed on paper that had yellowed with age and was beginning to crumble; equatorial humidity is ruinous to books. According to published histories, an Aaron Simonovich was either Rasputin's personal secretary or a shadier figure at the Imperial court.

They left St. Petersburg because of the Revolution. After many travels and adventures—Papa had another wife and a daughter in France—he ended up in an internment camp during World War Two. Freed by the British army, he joined it, and after the war he walked across the Sahara Desert to Liberia, where naturally he went into the restaurant business. I believed every word of the stories they told in that smaller version of Rick's Café, far down the coast from Casablanca.

But now, forty years later, I asked myself why my mother wanted me to tell this story. And this is what I decided:

The story demonstrated her own place in a vast network of mothers. They lived in every part of the world—from Poland and the Ukraine; to the towns in Massachusetts where my mother was born, raised her family, ran a business, and died a few years ago; to Vienna—even to a small, humid seaport on the African coast. And whatever else happens in this world, good or bad—where we travel, how we live, whatever new bonds we form—all the mothers everywhere sing these songs to us—and keep us together.

Because we remember.

Sarah Glenn Fortson

I Will Remember Now

I forgot, for awhile,
 to dream
of that cottage
with the screen door
of trillium blooms
of banjo tunes
and ferns on a forest floor
of slick laurel leaves
the rhododendron trees
and water falling over rock
the scent of damp shaded wood
and how tall the white pine stood.
I forgot, for awhile,
to dream
of the fireflies light
on a warm summer night
and the way the frogs sang in the trees
I forgot the place
where butterflies gather
and big city worries
don't seem to matter,
where little white churches
are at road's end
and watermelon drips down my chin
where every leaf and log
is set just right
and the barn owls hoot
at night
where moss grows green,
bears grow strong
and mother nature
is never wrong.
I forgot, for awhile,
to dream of that cottage
with the screen door
of trillium blooms

of banjo tunes
and ferns on a
forest floor.
but, I'll remember now,
to dream.
I'll remember now
like never before.
Dreams so precious and rare,
I'll remember now,
Because...
You were there.

ABOUT FACE

Exsulo Illustro

Level 101:

Critical thinker, mind drawn toward reason,
Subject all to analysis, else cognitive treason,
Still thirst for heart's guidance across changing soul season.

Sampler of darkness, entranced by depth's song,
Consequence, great teacher, always ready with prong;
Returned now to light, perceive ancient lines drawn,
Truth stranger than fiction, hence few seek the dawn.

Rejecter of blindness perpetrated by clever upon sheep,
Overcome astral battles, energetic victories reap,
Defenses persist, even while grounded in sleep.

See past illusion, architect's fist within glove,
Shift time penetrated, quiet push turned to shove;
Achilles' heel below extends to above,
Monocular servants shall never comprehend love.

Elayne Clift

Writing My Mother's Life

"I want you to have my typewriter," my mother said one day in 1991 from her nursing home bed. Not "Take my typewriter," as in "Take my jewelry. I won't need it anymore." This time she said, "I want you to have my typewriter." Then she said, "I want you to write the story." By then, "the story" in her mind was about nurses poisoning her and conspiracies of cruelty. I promised to tell the story. Not that one, of course, but her real story.

I had known for a long time that I needed to tell the story of my mother's life so that I could reconcile it and in so doing, put an end to sadness. At first I thought I'd have to gather more facts. I would go in search of an oral history, I thought, and in her roots and her childhood, finally discover my mother and make sense of her life.

Until then I thought of my mother's life as one story. Now I understand that the telling of her life is really two stories. The cruelty of that reality is that they can never be reconciled.

The first story is a kind of fiction; it contains the facts. Reba was born near Odessa in The Ukraine in 1904 sometime preceding the High Holy Days of Rosh Hoshana. In the absence of documentation, her birthday was celebrated annually on August 25th. Her given name was Brona in Hebrew but she chose to be called Reba while growing up in small town, anglicized New Jersey where she had emigrated at the age of two. Her father, Samuel-the-tailor, was stingy with love in the years of her growing up, but her beloved mother, Ida, was devoted. As my mother matured they became friends, a tragedy in the end, for my maternal grandmother died by her own hand at the age of fifty-two after her three children were grown.

Reba was a good student but, needing to work, she went from eighth grade to secretarial school, where she excelled. After graduation, she worked for a prestigious law firm in Camden, NJ, until her boss propositioned her with a strand of French pearls and a litany of promises, forcing her to move on.

One could understand his attraction. My mother was a beauty whose burning black eyes held an aura of mystery. When I was young, I cherished a photograph of her swathed in pastel pink and blue, those dark, piercing eyes framed by rich brunette curls cascading down her shoulders. There was another equally stunning photograph in which my mother is wearing green satin and velvet lounging pajamas. Posing seductively, she looks like a young, glamorous Indira Gandhi. There's no doubt about it: my mother had real class.

She was also talented, energetic, and full of humor and high hopes—in short, everybody's dream girl. And that is why she began contributing to her own fiction.

Douglas G. Campbell

I Don't Stand Up When They Play Dixie

In corridors
where lockers bang
as books slap down hard on metal,
where tongues whisk in and out of mouths
snake-like and slippery
slyly bragging
"Ours is the last all-white class."
Next year would the graduation gowns
be all-white like ours?
Would they run the field's length
carrying the stars and bars
before football games?
Will butts and asses
rise from those hard bleacher seats
as strains of Dixie charge through
open fields skirting that one state capitol
never conquered by Yankees
like me?

Karen de Balbian Verster

Answered Prayers

Writing this book is like climbing up to the top of a very high diving platform and seeing this little, tiny, postage-stamp-size pool below. To climb back down the ladder would be suicide. The only thing to do is to dive in with style.

-Truman Capote

My spiritual journey really began when my atheist father was dying of metastasized prostate cancer. Dad, who was extremely intelligent – a scientist and self-taught computer maven – but emotionally a bit retarded, loved to bait people, particularly religious people (the more devout, the better) in order to show them once and for all how misguided they were. My mother recounts (with the relish of one who is just so glad the story isn't about *her*) how Dad once reduced a South American exchange student to tears at a cocktail party because the young man made the mistake of espousing some Catholic dogma.

So Dad on his death-bed, all wan and tuckered out like a dog panting in the sun, says, "God has forsaken me." He utters this soap opera sentiment triumphantly and mockingly, with a bit of sly curiosity as to my reaction.

Raised an atheist, I'd never laid eyes on a Bible, nor attended church except once when a neighbor re-kindled my mother's tamped down agnosticism with visions of my tender soul burning in hell and convinced her to let me attend church with her family one Sunday. I must've evinced some enjoyment (perhaps I was just so glad to be with a merry group of affectionate people) because sometime thereafter, Dad dropped me off at the door of a church seemingly picked at random, apparently so he'd be off the hook if I did indeed burn in hell.

I was about ten and I sat alone in the pew wearing my lacy party dress and black patent leather Mary Janes like the proverbial atheist at his funeral – all dressed up and no place to go, not knowing what to do and feeling that everyone was staring at me. (They probably were.) I felt so alienated by the whole experience that my burgeoning spirituality was completely extinguished. (Could Dad have been that Machiavellian?)

When we moved to the buckle of the Bible belt, I suffered through school prayer and the inevitable Southern who-are-your-people-what-church-do-you-attend introductions. After escaping to Manhattan, I led a dissipated life by most standards, although I felt quite the liberated woman. I remained steadfast in my cynicism about God and the people who believed in him until, in my mid-thirties, I quit trying to fill my God-sized hole with alcohol, and became open to the idea of a Higher Power.

"Maybe you have forsaken him," I tentatively reply to my dying father.

My budding spiritual awareness is no match for Dad, a fire-breathing atheist whose passion was presumably ignited by the priest who tried to grope him when he was a boy.

"That's a crock of shit!" Dad says with surprising ferocity. He closes in for the kill, savoring this moment in an almost orgasmic fashion. "First of all, there is no God. But if there were, it would be a She, because only a woman could fuck things up this badly."

Dad went to his grave at least outwardly an atheist, and I went on to have three breast cancer diagnoses. Unaccountably, illogically, the closer to death I got, the more I believed in God and I thanked Him for this "growth" opportunity (amusing myself with the pun), since it provided the impetus for my novel, *Boob, A Story of Sex, Cancer & Stupidity*. As Fénelon wrote in the seventeenth century, "I am amazed at the power that comes to us through suffering... Of course, I tremble and agonize while it lasts, and all my words about the beneficial effects of suffering vanish under the torture. But when it is all over, I look back on the experience with deep appreciation, and am ashamed that I bore it with so much bitterness."

Before my first cancer diagnosis (Stage II), my relationship with God was dodgy —trying to ignore Dad's cynical voice in my head while attempting to pray was like having a whispered conversation with the TV blaring— and unsatisfyingly cerebral as I self-consciously prayed for God to help me feel His presence. I finally resorted to the ploy of "acting as if" I believed in God, which conjured images of Jimmy Stewart and his friend, Harvey, the six-foot rabbit.

It was also hard for me to separate Dad's cancer from my own since both struck at the outward symbols of our genders. I was driven by what he didn't do: he didn't change his diet, his attitudes, his lifestyle. Shortly before he died, I bought him a bunch of self-help books. The only one he wanted was Elizabeth Kubler-Ross's *On Death and Dying*. I returned the rest to the bookstore since it didn't occur to me to read them myself. After Dad died, his wife gave me the Kubler-Ross book, along with some birthday cards I'd made him over the years. My therapist suggested that perhaps I got cancer as a way to be closer to my father.

I had a hard time asking for help, but when I was in the hospital I was forced to rely on my husband for assistance. This turned out to be beneficial since I was all outgoing energy with very little room for incoming, healing energy. Slowly, the enormous burden of self-sufficiency slid from my

105

shoulders and I gave myself up to being taken care of, loved and nurtured by my husband. It was a facet of our relationship I'd never experienced since I'd made him into a father figure who ultimately was going to let me down. I learned that the willingness to allow others to help me was an essential part of my recovery.

I'd already made most of the diet and exercise changes that people make *after* they're diagnosed, so I decided something else was required of me, something spiritual in nature. Cancer occurs when the immune system fails to destroy cancer cells (present in everyone's body), and stress depresses the immune system. What most effectively relieved stress for me was a belief in God whom I tried to access through yoga and qigong, prayer and meditation. But after the doctors pronounced me "cured," I lost the sense of urgency that had previously propelled me.

Five years after my first cancer diagnosis, my mother gave me a dozen red roses to celebrate my victory. Seven months later, while slogging through my journals in search of material to use in my novel (an unexpectedly painful process since I could perceive and feel things I wasn't able to while in dog-paddle survivor mode), I found a lump in my breast. Hoping it was all a mistake—silly goose, panicking over some fatty tissue—I was devastated when its presence was confirmed by my oncologist.

As I walked home, fearing death while simultaneously entertaining the idea of throwing myself in front of a cab, the sky darkened and I thought, *I guess I'm not such a good person after all. The spiritual work I've done has all been in vain. I've barely scratched the surface—like those bone-wielding apes in 2001—of my monolithic ego. I'm hopeless and I'm going to die a slow and agonizing death.*

I dreaded returning to my surgeon and having to fight my way through the medical morass yet again as I strove to receive treatment that was warranted rather than gratuitous. I was beginning to be daunted by all these male authority figures who seemed to represent my father in one guise or another, while, at the other end of the spectrum, God became the ultimate male authority figure whose censure and condemnation I feared as well.

"I can't go through this again," I wailed to a friend. "I don't have the strength."

"The last time this happened you didn't have the strength to deal with it right away," my friend said. "You cried. And then you got strong."

I prayed over and over that God's will be done. What *was* God's will? Was it for me to be an example to others, like my friend who had courageously died of ovarian cancer? Or was this just another spiritual goose? I realized the first time I'd battled cancer, I'd white-knuckled it. I'd believed if I just read enough, did enough, changed enough, I could impact the outcome. And it appeared I had. Now I saw how ultimately powerless I was over cancer, and that the only way I could truly overcome it was to get out of the way so I could avail myself of God's love and wisdom.

I was determined to stick around for my daughter whom I'd had in between my two diagnoses despite going into premature menopause as a result of chemotherapy, but I felt a great deal of anxiety at the idea of leaving her against my will. I called a spiritual friend to talk about death who said, "Your daughter is in God's hands. If you die, she'll be taken care of. And you'll be re-united. It may feel like a long time to you now, but in the hereafter it's a blink of an eye."

"You know, just before I got this diagnosis, I had the greatest equanimity about death, and now I'm terrified."

"Let me read you a quote from *The Urantia Book*," he said. "'Even if I cannot do this, there lives in me one who can and will do it, a part of the Father-Absolute of the universe of universes.' Pray for the removal of fear, for peace. God may not be able to grant your every request, but the one thing he will grant immediately and unconditionally is peace of mind. This is how the cosmos evolves — every time someone squarely faces a problem and calls on God's help."

I decided to begin yet another cancer makeover entailing heavy-duty God contact, severe dietary cutbacks, and plenty of service to others to take my mind off of me, me, me. The God stuff helped. On the days, usually toward the late afternoon, when I fell into despair, I put my pedal to the metal and roared down the divine highway. Within a couple of hours, the mood lifted and I could resume functioning.

At a spiritual workshop, Sister Maurice said, "God will give us what we ask our daily bread— but it's just enough for today. We have to live today to its fullest and begin again the next day."

"I just keep thinking I don't want to die. I want to live to be one hundred and four."

"When we die it means our work here is done."

"But I don't feel my work is done, not with my daughter only three, and my book unpublished. But hey, God's will is stronger than mine when it comes to death."

Or was it? I tried to winnow out my negative, complacent victim thoughts — was there a part of me that wanted to die, wanted to be cut up, tortured with chemo? Like a person who has decided on suicide, I contemplated how everyone would miss me when I was gone, their sorrow at my memorial, the glowing tributes. *And yet,* I thought, *I'd really rather publish my books, give readings, and receive the accolades pre-humously. More will be revealed. I'm not dying today.*

After finding a third lump above my collar bone a year later (which earned me a Stage IV diagnosis), I accidentally scalded my chest which served as a reminder how often I used physical pain as a stand-in for emotional pain. There were big chunks of my childhood I couldn't remember, and evidence pointing to sexual abuse, possibly from my father, but would knowing the exact details alleviate the pain? I had tried that with my first diagnosis. Knew every detail of my pathology report and what it signified. Knew all the statistics. By the third one (like the third child of whom there are no baby pictures), I didn't even read the pathology report. Even so, I felt I wouldn't be cured until I unraveled the mystery of what my body was harboring.

I dreamed I was watching a group of women on a hillside. They were using a piece of farm equipment, perhaps a combine. I realized they were mermaids. Suddenly, they all turned toward the sea as a large man rose from the water. In place of a penis was an octopus, tightly furled. "Let her go, let her go," they cried. He walked ashore and the mermaids got him by the legs and held him with the machinery. Slowly, the octopus unfurled its tentacles and the man removed a mermaid from its grasp. He let her go.

My qigong instructor showed the class some exercises that would reverse the effects of aging.

"Yeah, but will they make you live longer?" I asked.

The instructor, a Chinese man, looked at me in surprise. "That is not important," he said. "What matters is how you live each day."

Hmmph, I sniffed to myself. *That's easy for you to say. You don't have a life-challenging disease.*

But his viewpoint was confirmed in Harriet and Malcolm Beinfield's thought-provoking paper, "Revisiting Accepted Wisdom in the Management of Breast Cancer," whose last paragraph stated, "Buddhists claim that life is an evolutionary exercise in learning lessons dressed in suffering. One antidote to suffering is glad acceptance — not wishing for things to be other than they are." At some point during the repeated viewings of the first plane hitting the World Trade Center during the 2001 terrorist attack, I thought, "I wish I'd been on that plane." Even though I'd been cancer-free for a number of years, there was something appealing about sudden death, and the cessation of all my doubts and fears it would bring.

That's what it's like to get a cancer diagnosis. You're walking along and it's a peerless day — clear blue skies, temps in the seventies. The last thing on your mind is the thought of attack. Then BAM! The planes collide, the buildings collapse and nothing will ever be the same. You can't ever really enjoy a peerless day again, because every time you hear a plane it might be a terrorist. Every time you get a headache it might be cancer.

How do you live a life without a future? That's the conundrum of cancer. You have to be willing to die, to live. If you're all stressed out and fearful that you might get another diagnosis, all that stress and fear make you more susceptible to getting another diagnosis. If you have faith that God will take care of you, you might still die, but at least you won't be all stressed out and fearful. As C.S. Lewis wrote, "Submit to death, death of your ambitions and favorite wishes every day and death of your whole body in the end: submit with every fiber of your being, and you will find eternal life."

Dorothy Stone

Two Looks Back

Evolution in a Marriage
1961 to 2---

A curl of smoke
a wispy cloud
blown about.

A collection of stories,
ideas, dreams,
but where is the clip
to hold them
together?

Row after row
of question mark
after question mark
crowds out
any fresh-faced answers.

A fire refusing
to be quenched
finally dares
conflagration
in hope of new growth.

A profusion of flowers
unexpected
planted forgotten
springs up within.

An antique trunk
treasures intact
secrets, pictures,

memories, dreams.
The family's store.
The family core.

Snapshots from One Woman's Album

Me —the "Big Day"

Why am I here in this filmy white cloud?
Veils soften edges but then blur one's sight.
Is he Prince Charming? And if not, who am I?
Sun cloud or rain cloud or wisp blown about?
Weak-kneed I bow to the winds in control,
leaving it all up to fate and to chance.

New York: Ten Years! (Can you find me?)

My neighborhood, yes, no doubt it is mine,
the deli, the laundry, both tell me it is;
but as in a dream, I wander about,
feel myself lost on this urban earth.
The wind comes up swiftly, blows my papers about.
My task, to save them, to scoop them all up:
frantic I clutch at the mess of my life,
torn fragments of meanings no more making sense.
"But mine! But me," I shout into the gale.
Can I hold them together? Resist the storm's blast?
Save marriage and husband and child—and myself?

WE LEAVE THE CITY—Solution?   Beginning of the End?

Dawn on the prairie, the sky covers all.
How long since I left? And why come again?
Were ancestors filled with such hard questions too?
And was hope strong enough to outweigh their fear?
"What am I doing here?" inward I cry.
That question alone does not need to be asked:
I needed a home. Dawn's promise. My sky.

Back East! Me Gambling—All or Nothing! Everything on the Red.

Unfocused shot with too little light:
The tiny glow flickers, too dim, too dim.
Add candles, more candles, dispensing some gloom.

112

Candelabra takes over, the anger does too.
The whole batch I tip, my breath fans the flames,
and the old is consumed to make room for new growth.

We Start Over—Our New Home

Wild flowers bloom instead of plain grass;
perennial renewal, not plotted nor planned,
surprises us both who thought we'd seen all.
The daisies, the lilies, the violets, too,
pop up unexpected, their pattern their own,
attracting the bees, outsinging the birds,
slaked by the clouds, fed by the sun.

The End? Hardly!

An antique trunk sits under our stairs,
my grandmother's companion as she approached a new land.
It held what she valued, preserves what I've kept;
it protects who I was and who I became
and saves me for now and tomorrows to come.

Nancy Skalla

Sounds of a Woman's Growth

Babies cried – so did the bills and pressure for dollars blared - bring more in! Our insatiable ledger always starved for cash; negatives and payments on hold. Solutions were grim with no car for travel, no infant care, and absence of training for work. Excuses made little difference while dollars screamed for more.

Tires plus key lifted a gate, however - infants still young. Star wheels and key punch changed the scene, but training lagged behind. Class at noon? I could try, but what of the children and cost? Moms frozen out of gain - missing vital school, missing experience and care - yet the dollars continued to scream, we need more.

Guts of a corporate move spurred me on. Backward leaning he rocked - beard and pipe looking smug. "Go home; take care of your children. Our training's not meant for women your age." Schoolcraft College closed their door; now attitudes lagged behind. I stared and swallowed with anger and fear- too stupid to know how to scream.

One more move with global shift of breadwinners large and small. Older kids meant training went forward; but dollars still hollered their need. With years raising kids - could I still count? The bank interview suit pressed. Bonnie sat next and intervened. In our country, sir, women do all. She softly screamed on my behalf, "Yes, she still can count."

He said, "No" to job and cash. Stunned at my energies of waste, I argued my work in real estate sales and class of accounting columns; but still he said "no" to job and cash. Word processor typed a message of bias – how much must we do? Instruction...experiences still not enough, but at last I was learning to scream.

Thank you for censure, it makes us strong. Sleep needs get small and worry does too. No longer will suit or beard tell me no - as I walk with degree in hand. But years are passing; marketability fades. Hearth is important no matter the cost, opportunities thin to compare. Are my ears getting numb to the screams?

Family raised - unspoiled by wealth – often craving provisions of style. Their protein was that of learning; vitamins filled by ethic and love; water for growth from new Web. The call for money gave me a goal, but the effort returned so much more. I gained fodder of mind, strength of voice and deafness to trifling screams.

Nicole Zimmerman

Shasta in Stanzas

When he returned from the summit, she curled up next to his frostbitten toe. He said the wilderness teaches you about your own resilience.

She watched her firefighter-river-guide-mountaineer unpack his coiled ropes and carabineers. I'm a man of commitment, honesty and love, he announced.

Later he would light the woodstove and make stir-fry while she wept.

He would putter around his yard. This is where the fishpond will go, he said, pointing next to the Magnolia he'd planted for her.

They would walk along the bluff and watch the sun change shape. They did not touch in the almost darkness. She listened to him discuss the weather while she beseeched the stars.

Then one day he fell in love with someone else.

She saw the evidence everywhere: the barrettes on the bathroom counter, the little bike out front. A mosaic steppingstone of the mountain lay not far from the Magnolia tree.

We even share the same dreams, he told her, forgetting that it wasn't the first time.

She consoled herself with pots of soup and hovered by the heater over a long winter. In spring she drove to the snow-covered crag as flocks of red-winged blackbirds flew from the dawn.

At dusk the snowy peaks glowed purple. Her tent was a silhouette, wrapped in the shadow of twilight.

Heavy winds blew down as she fell into dreams. That was God's breath clearing everything out, someone said in the morning.

Outside, a sliver of moon still hung in the sky.

Dave Morrison

Namesake

There were, as far as I knew,
no Davids in my family. My mother
named me after King David, in the Bible.

When I was small she would sing this song
that went "Little David, play on your harp-"
which I assumed meant that I was supposed

to blow harmonica in a blues band, but I
don't think that's what she'd intended. I didn't
know who I was supposed to be.

Mostly I grew to suspect that I had a
lot of work to do if I was ever going to
be accepted by God. There was

one narrow road one had to
walk, and I kept
wandering off of it.

I was taught to avoid sex and violence, but the
Bible was chock-full of it. In fact, my namesake,
who seemed to relish war, got one of his soldier's

wives pregnant, and then arranged for
the man to be killed on the battlefield. This
is where I got confused; I believed that the

tiniest infraction was intolerable to God, yet
King David could have sex with another man's wife and
have him killed and still be loved by the Lord –

if we went to the wrong church, or drank or smoked
cigarettes we would be locked out of heaven.
Our sins were puny but exacted a high price-

how could the murder and betrayal in the
Bible somehow score lower than my doubt
and vulgarity and confusion on God's shit list?

King David played a stringed instrument and
eventually so did I, but he played for sheep and
kings, and I played in bars, so that offered no clue.

Finally I realized why I had been named for
him, and it had nothing to do with my mother or
Sunday School or Goliath; God bless him, David was

a poet. He sinned mightily, but he wrote the psalms,
and had a bold heart, and I imagine he was doing the
best he knew how, as who he was.

It began to make sense, I
began to make sense.
My cup runneth over.

Nancy Lubarsky

What If, As Your Sister Claimed

(For My Father)

*A thing may happen and be a total lie; another thing
may not happen and be truer than the truth.*

        - Tim O'Brien, The Things They Carried

What if you were never on that battleship, as
your sister claimed, when she heard your voice

on the tape I mailed to her after your funeral?
What if you never went to the latrine—there

was no explosion, no friends left behind on
the deck, no shrapnel in your leg? What if

you hadn't spent months in a hospital, tending
the gash that she argued was from an accident

in your father's bakery? What if there was
no purple heart—you didn't give it away to

a stranger? That day we talked for hours; I
recorded it all. Years later my friend asked

if I was curious about what really happened,
but I already knew. It was a war story.

Alan Cohen

Here Comes Dad, 1947

I hear him hacking half a block away
Dad's wrenching sounds careening off
the brick-lined concrete valley we call
our stickball court where no-bounce past
Mr. Wiley's Chevrolet is worth two bases
but yellow hydrant is out of bounds

one hand's palm against brick walls he
climbs the hill the other waves *The Boston
Post* signaling **I have Nancy and Her
Friends Brenda Starr and sports pages too**
while I feign not noticing he clutches
his chest and pops another nitro as

he pauses to catch oxygen-starved breath
finally lifting him to the hilltop and then
three flights to where he sinks into his chair
dozing until supper time and Ma whispering
shhh you'll wake your dad
family code for a heart worn threadbare

in childhood innocence I didn't know but
toward the end I learned the game and
played it well one step behind him never
asking **can I help you up the stairs** or
**will you die and never talk to me
again about the Boston Red Sox**

Ahrend R. Torrey

Boy

   Grab a chain out back of the old Ford; go down to Frost Bridge and help Curt pull his truck out of the gully; make sure you attach the chain right; don't pull too hard, you might damage the axle; try to be quick; remember to take your sister to youth group; make sure you pick up a couple twelve-packs, your mom is throwing another party; never climb a tree with your gun loaded; never take shit from anybody; if it's fight or walk away, you fight; always respect your elders even when they're in the wrong; never associate with fags, that's what comes of the sissy you are bent on becoming; don't get a car, trucks are more useful; don't let your mother find your magazines, you don't want her to know the truth to why you always lock the door; when pink is the only color, find another; go to the garage and help bring in groceries; wear a condom though it takes a little time; is it true that your lotion is next to the fruit basket?; don't forget to take out the trash, the paper said the garbage pick-up date has changed, don't forget; never use nails for sheetrock; never use yellow PVC on toilets, that pipe is for hot water, not cold; don't leave your lotion on the kitchen counter; this is how you work like a man; this is how you sweat, unlike the sissy you are bent on becoming; this is how you lift weights; this is how you talk dirty; this is how you never bait a hook; this is how you look like a gentleman; *but that isn't my lotion; why would I put it next to the fruit basket?;* this is how you tough it up; this is how you laugh at dirty jokes; this is how you take a dip, always keeping a spit-cup wherever you go; this is how you demand more than your share, because the world will screw you in the end, you have to keep ahead; open the door for Ms. Edna; try and be home before twelve; pen-up Jake before the neighbors shoot him he keeps getting in the trash; this is how you catch a football; this is how you make a trail; this is how you make a trail when you don't have a machete; this is how you make a trail when you don't need to make a trail at all; this is how you throw a baseball; this is how you fall in love; this is who you love; this is how you fall out of love; this is how you grease a motor; this is how you take a risk; this is how you appear hard, when everyone's against you; this is how you fail; this is how you fail and never cry; this is how you fail and get up again; this is how you call a duck; this is how to skin a buck; this is how you aim correctly as not to spook the turkey; this is how you play guitar; this is how to run a bar; this is how you change oil because quick lubes over-charge; experience is the best way to pass mechanic school; *but what if I don't want to be a mechanic, but a violinist?* You mean to say after all, boy, you want to be the sissy I've tried so hard to keep you from becoming?

Nan Rush

I Dress in Red

Tell Me Your Life

(For Dan)

Tell me your life,
he says,
as we sit baking
on the sundeck
at my parents' home
and I say, well, bro,
I rehearse, write, read,
see my son two times a week,
and work.
That's it.

I think he expects
something more from me –
that I've walked a tightrope
from the PP&L building to
the other side of the street,
drank a fifth of bourbon
in one night then
came home and wrote
a screenplay
drunk with dialog,
that I belong to wildness.

I wake in the morning
and stretch, think –
another day,
another way to dress,
to walk into the world
without getting arrested.

He sees me as outlaw,

wild,
not reticent,
while I feel so humbled
lately by the blows
I've been fed
I feel lucky to just
be here,
not dead,

but I will fuel his
imagination,
and dress in red
for him.

Scrapbook

Old play programs,
newspaper photographs,
locks of hair,
poems written and long forgotten,
breaths drawn in and exhaled,
captured in a scrapbook.

My life is a scrapbook
composed of barely recognizable me's,
me doing this,
me saying that,
me running through places
I can't remember.

If you knew me then,
do you remember me now?
If you saw me now,
would you remember me then?
Would my face recall the
me you used to know?
Would I remember you?

I have no locks of your hair.
I have no pictures of you.
The only thing that brings you
home to me
are songs we both knew.

I can't recapture your face,
your touch,
the man you once were,
the man who moved me so much
I thought I'd left this world for heaven.

Now I don't believe in that.
Now I think heaven is
the dream of yesterday —
seeing my aunt smile
when I'd walk through her door,

smelling my grandmother's rhubarb pie,
feeling the tall grass kiss my thighs
in a field now plowed under.

Changing the Mantle

(Prose Poem)

I think of changing the mantle above my fireplace. It's crowded and doesn't make any sort of artistic statement.

I'll get rid of the candles, the incense, the pictures, and leave it stark – one seashell, one flower, or a pair of old shoes. Or maybe something I've beaten to death – My Aunt Moogs' pants from the forties, or the only picture of my lover that he let me take.

No, something else, something not him: a picture I drew in college, a nude from my art class, before I knew the body, the secrets within. Or piles of antique books.

Yes! I'll make the mantle a bookcase, since I've run out of room on my shelves. Or maybe a shrine to the Beatles: my Flip Your Wig game, John and Jeremy figures from Yellow Submarine, old vinyl albums, and a hand painted sign saying "God Save the Queen."

I'm not afraid to change things, to experiment with the appearance of my world. In my youth, I may have doubted my skill at dress, worrying about whether I'd make the right impression. But underneath that, I was fearless, I guess – I did it anyway. And still do today: Vote Choice stickers on my car after my address was posted on the Internet by the Missionaries to the Unborn.

I flaunt my loves, my dreams, my beliefs, despite my fear. Otherwise, life becomes a chore, my fireplace mantle's a bore, and I won't believe anymore that I have a choice, that I can change things.

Stroking the Ghosts

I stroke the ghosts
of loves lost,
and they moan
and vibrate at my touch.

I stroke the ghosts
as they climb
into my fresh bed
and whisper –
"Let me sink
under the covers
with you
and hide
from the thunder
and lightning."

I stroke the ghosts
of myself:
me at nine,
not chosen as anyone's partner
for the Halloween Parade
(maybe that's why
Masquerade parties are
so vital to me now);
me at ten,
good only as the
smart one
to be copied from;
me at twelve,
silenced when
I innocently told
of being taken
advantage of
by a relative;
me at sixteen,
alone in the house,
hysterical from rejection
by my first love.
I stroke the ghosts

at midnight,
and
the low hum
of their voices

keeps me
from
sleep.

My Hands

I look at my hands.
They are not hands
like my grandfather's,
that built houses,
or painted pictures
of planes and Presidents
and progeny, like my father's,
or sewed dresses & blouses &
skirts like my mother's.

They are Piano Hands,
someone once told me.
A boyfriend said
they made him want to cry
(I never did know why).
Now my left hand aches and bears a
bulbous protrusion on the pad,
starting to hamper the Chopin stretches.
Too much typing, or arthritis
inherited?

My Uncle Frank had terrible hands,
swollen, distorted from that disease.
I can't imagine his pain, his unease,
yet always, he laughed,
told stories that slayed
his audience (so infectious
a laugh he had).

Yes, my left hand in piano has
begun to go bad,
and turning pages hurts
whenever I read.
The skin, if hydrated,
can fight off wrinkles,
but still I wonder why

did that boyfriend want to cry,
looking at my hands?
They touched him.
They stretched to circle his heart.

Barbara Tatro

Mannequin

It is late. The house long since deserted. The bed is cold. I draw the comforter around me and wait for sleep to come. My mind begins to drift like an unmanned craft catching each wind and swell it happens upon. And, sleep does not come.

I search for the justice within my reverie. I conjure systems devised for matching children with parents. Maybe a poker draw or perhaps a decision spat out by a ghostly Jekyll and Hyde who lurks about in the shadows of time. Who or what has been given this power?

A window rattles in its frame, bringing me back to myself. I wonder how much time has passed. I close my eyes and am transported to that house. I make my way through the dark, recalling the smells, hearing again the creaks and groans. I stop and turn. I am seven. I see my father. I feel tension and taste bitterness. My body is stiff and cold. I wonder what he is thinking as he sensually caresses legs skinned and bruised from the games a little girl plays. His eyes narrow to slits. He fixes his gaze. His lip twitches and he says, "I love you."

And he came, a thief in the night, to rob me of my trust, my innocence, and my dignity.

And now, it is morning breaking through the window that separates past from present. I realize that it is the hand of fate that defines love. Those who know love as it was meant to be shake their heads and pass judgment on the promiscuous ones hewn of stone.

We, on the other hand, undress in the night, lay in the dark, and wait for love to come.

Carol J. Rhodes

Big Shoes to Fill

In retrospect, I may have had more fun out of life if I hadn't been so concerned about order and appearances, if I had just vacuumed the traffic paths and let the rest go. But given my background, there were big shoes, shined to perfection, to be filled.

Mamie Potter

The Golf Course Grass

The first time you sat on the country club golf course it was winter and everyone brought mason jars filled with gin and vodka and bourbon from their parents' liquor cabinets. You were cold and glad for the hot burn: your first taste of booze. You shuddered, swallowed to keep the nasty liquid down, and raised the jar to your mouth again.

In the summer, you laid on this grass with your boyfriend, smoking Old Gold cigarettes and making out. Warm enough to raise your shirt and pull your shorts down to give you more skin to skin. You got your first French kiss under this bordering tree, the thick thrust of his tongue disgusting but exciting too.

At one of the country club dances, you sat on the grass in the dark and cried while the bastard who bought your corsage and your dinner danced with the blond whose father ran the bank. Her family belonged to the club and yours didn't and you knew then that it mattered, but not why.

Home from college you smoked pot on the grass, smoked grass on the grass, hilarious, a slap in the face of the members of the club, your jeans and your moccasins a far cry from the taffeta dance dress with the blue-dyed shoes.

Tonight it's your tenth reunion, it's at the club, and in the car with two guys from your class you smoked cigarettes and dope and drank moonshine from a jar. Now you lie alone with your dress pulled up; the night air moves across your feet and your legs and you savor the cool, damp itch of the grass.

Terry Martin

In the Space Provided Below, Tell Us About Yourself

After learning to dress myself, tie my shoes, and read,
I earned merit badges, diagrammed sentences,
sang second soprano in the choir.
Built hundreds of campfires by Coeur d 'Alene Lake
where I took full, deep breaths.
Attended three universities, accumulated student loans,
kissed nineteen different guys one summer in Guadalajara.
Listened to Aretha belt out "R-E-S-P-E-C-T."
Fell in love, fell out of love, fell in love again.
Cooked spicy pork stew, adding extra garlic and jalapenos.
Lied to myself, then tried not to any more.
Wore five different uniforms; outgrew all but one.
Held my mother's hand as she died. Didn't have children.
Heard a sail luffing, flapping its empty dream.
Hurt someone badly along the way.
Watched old women on porches in Bruge, tatting lace.
Found a good teacher. Quit biting my fingernails.
Lost seventy pounds, gained twenty back.
Rotated my tires, but not often enough.
Re-read *A Tree Grows in Brooklyn,*
wept for the things I didn't know.
Danced to the end of the page, then
over the margins into other stories.
Dreamed fence posts and barbed-wire
far into the horizon.

Ongoing Conversation

Dear Jim,

Thinking of you, and your fasting. Of Karen, and her weight loss goals.
Of food, and our relationship to it. Yes.

The body.

A year and eight months ago, shortly after my breakdown (breakthrough!)
I remember my therapist saying: "Terry, your body is more than a vehicle
to carry your brain around. You're going to meet your body and get to
know it." I wondered.

Then I started doing my work. My real work.

We never talked about weight.
Not once.

We worked on the disconnect of feelings.
That blocking. What it does to the body.
Analysis over feeling.
Filtering.
The sadness, the longing.
Hungry Ghosts.

And the push.
The drive.
The striving.

Making friends with all of it.

I'm still working on it. I'll always be working on it, I think.

Then, a year ago January, I began to make the connection.
Body as temple (not amusement park!).
It was just time.
Cancer had something to do with it of course:
Jane's. My mom's, too. (I was turning forty-six—the age she had been
when she was diagnosed).

And peri-menopause was part of it, too.
Cut off from my usual protections.
The anxiety, edginess, moodiness, insomnia as my way in, as the door…
Hot flashes, too. Wild, wild rides. Unbelievable.
When the heat comes, how to use its force to burn through to awareness.
What do I want transformed?

Began listening to what my body wanted, to what it needed:
Stretching.
The daily walk. (Now, four 15-minute miles.)
Healthy food, smaller portions.
No caffeine.

Less.

Started asking: What is my actual energy vs. my will?
Radical.

Connecting up the parts.

She was right. I'm meeting my body, and getting to know it.
To like it, even.

Losing the first fifty pounds wasn't hard. These last fifteen are slow going,
though.

It's doing my real work that's been hard.

As the push eases in me,
It eases from me, to others…

I'm off to my therapist Wednesday.

We don't talk about weight.

Summer DeNaples

For Painter and Brides

Imagine you are a painter about to reveal your first piece.
Critic: It's okay. It needs yellow.
You add a little (meticulously) and hang your work ready for its début.
When you return for the unveiling ceremony,
You find that he has added more yellow in your absence.
It looks beautiful yes, but—
My painting was my wedding, and the critic an event planner.
Had I not spent so many hours on the aesthetic—
New Mother-in-Law (and everyone else for that matter): no one is going to
care about the details
Me (between sobs): I already feel stupid without your help
After seeing me, one maid of honor says
That she will not put as much effort into her wedding,
I try to imagine not caring.
The other maid of honor says
That we've made a believer out of her.
The wedding is an unstoppable force,
Speeches, Champaign, dancing,
And people love it.
They say they see us in the details.
The painter image leaves out an important component:
The groom,
Who actually worked as hard as I did on the aesthetic, didn't cry.
Instead, he told me: I want to be sympathetic,
But I am so happy.

Beth Lynn Clegg

The Four-Poster

He discovered the massive antique bed in the back room of his grandmother's antique shop. Running as fast as his eight-year-old legs would carry him, he scrambled up the small stepladder placed along side. Squeals of delight filled the building as he inspected his birthday gift and bounced on the old ticking mattress. Blankets and sheets draped over the tester frame created a hideaway for dreaming dreams and games of pretend.

As years passed, the bed became an extension of his personality – unique, solid, towering intelligence. Despite its thousand pound weight, he hauled it to college. The bed became the center of attention in more than one residence during his journey into adulthood where he discovered drugs and sex, losing more than the tester in his search for identity, as I watched with growing concern.

After graduating with honors, he earned a law degree before fantasies became reality and voices took direction of his life. He should live near water. It would tell him what to do. Pursue a profession that would not harm others. Cleanse himself so his true destiny could be revealed. He should not listen to his family. They did not understand.

And we no longer did. But while we foolishly engaged in heated debate over appropriate action he divested himself of material possessions and moved to California, his last known destination.

The bed now blends into my surroundings. I often drape myself under sheets and blankets, drifting into a world of make-believe where I will find my son, like the tester, discarded and lost somewhere on the scrap-heap of humanity.

Susan Grier

Goodbye

The week I moved in with my new girlfriend after my husband and I split up, I got together one evening with some female friends. We were each supposed to bring something to read aloud to the group. I didn't have time to even think about it ahead of time, so I wrote this in the car, free-writing as fast as my pen could move (my girlfriend was driving):

Goodbye

Toxic house
Heavy breathing
Blasting TV
Chirping hearing aids
Football
Creaking chair
Hunting paraphernalia
Demanding little piece of shrimp
Green walls
Luxury bathroom
Killer of creativity
Intruder of journals
Gross deformed toenails
Smug face
Ruined holidays
Ruined vacations
Ruined meals
CNN
Raspy nose noises
Newspapers turned inside out
Trashed vehicle
Snot in shower
three-year old temperament
Lazy ass
Snoring on the sofa
Killer of dreams
Resentment, impatience, irritability
Testosterone machismo

Lies and deception
Dead grass, dead trees, dead marriage
Loneliness
Verbal abuse
Tension
Conflict
Insanity.

Beth Winegarner

Half Empty

I once loved a drunk who carried his beer
everywhere in a brown sack
tucked against his arm like a wing or a weapon.

His bedroom bristled with empty bottles.
Joints, smoked down to the nubs, scattered like insects.
At night I never knew who would wake up next to me,
the mean drunk or the sad little boy.
The next morning I would tell him:
each night it's like you leave me alone with a stranger.

But in that cold room his hands were two suns
warming my chilled skin.
When I shivered they pressed into me,
seeking folds of winter, uncreasing them.

Once you've loved a drunk, you learn the gestures,
the whole syntax of drinking and taking pains
to pass as normal, the relentless thirst.

And when you see one coming, you walk the other way.

Tamara W.

That Old Life

It happened, it just happened, we did it with our eyes closed and our minds swilled, and it was both brutal and beautiful, a rite of passage like face tattooing or tribal beating or celebrations marking the onset of menstruation. And it had been so many years since it happened, so many years since all of those nights I spent sleepwalking through those dimly lit clubs, naked, but for my costume and another girl's name, tempting men without faces to find me. It had been so many years since I was that girl with the bedroom eyes and the muscled thighs, who crooned out lies and coaxed lonely men out of their wallets, that she is a stranger to me now, a phantom I no longer recognize no matter how hard I stare at the shape of my frame in the mirror.

Of course there are moments when I am sure that I still lie with her bones in my mattress. Her stiffness can seize up my spine when the scent of a lover exhausted beside me carries me to a back room I had blocked. She holds me when I lie with a man I don't really want, or spoon feed myself pleasure because it is still a notion I don't quite really believe in. She coils my stomach when the craving for violence is particularly strong, or on nights when I can't seem to turn down a drink, or when I don't sleep for a while and taste the old chalk in my gums.

There are moments too when I worry that if I ever do find someone I love that part of my past will bleed into my future, that I will find the courage to recount what it felt like to be that girl on the stage, and he will resent his resemblance to the men at the table.

Mostly though as the years fade and my hair grays and my old body blurs from my memory, I find myself grasping for that girl out of something nostalgic, like the dull pain of a wound you miss after your body has healed. I am less afraid that the girl will resurface as I am afraid that maybe she won't, that I will never again be as deeply alive as I was in those years when I held my heart in the darkness, that I will never again find a place that felt as much like home as those clubs did.

Madeleine Beckman

A Great Pass

Hey kid, what are ya doing up so late?
Come down, keep your pop company.

No! don't change the channel,
I'm watchin' the game.

Hey, do your pop a big favor,
grab that gallon of butter pecan

from the freezer, don't forget a spoon
and maybe the walnuts in syrup.

He's stretched on the black leather couch,
a furniture monstrosity that sticks to your skin.

He imagines he's still the athlete he once was
pitching baskets, the only whitey on a black team.

I pull up the *Lay-Z-Boy* beside him. The chair
is a huge, hideous green *Naugahyde* thing.

We watch football reruns, but I'm OK,
despite not understanding the scoring.

Did you see that toss, did you see it! He's jubilant,
(doesn't see me picking out all the pecans) while

I'm watching him watching,
watching him passing.

Christine Donovan

Gathering Flowers in My Father's Garden

It was a stately old colonial on a corner lot, white with black shutters and a veranda that was surrounded by large columns, giving it that perfect New England look. It was our house, my father's childhood home and the only thing I really thought of as my family's place in the world.

There were better years when my father gardened, circling the house with roses, lilacs, tulips and my favorite, gladiolas. There were tomatoes and peppers and green beans tucked in between the flowers. In his early sobriety he became obsessed with the garden's perfection, making sure there were no weeds or unsightly growth along the edges of neat trim.

He would order me out to help him weed and prune. I was terrified of pulling out a plant instead of a weed and I used the clippers for what seemed like hours; it was not my first experience with the Great Santini. Even as I worked alongside him, frightened of his temper and rage, it was the only way to be close to him, to experience him.

This was a flower I came to treasure and the way I understood my father's love. This occasional beauty around the exterior of the house did not reveal the tragedies inside, or the way love was mostly thorny and brambled. My father drank and became the infamous Dr. Jekyll and Mr. Hyde. This is our story.

There was a coffee can next to the kitchen sink that was for garbage scraps, coffee grounds, slop from the kitchen drain. It was juicy, smelly and overflowing onto the counter. It was supposed to go outside to the bucket that got picked up with the trash collection but it was emptied infrequently and sat there like a pitiful metaphor for all that was going on in our house: the foul odor of Dad's whiskey breath, the multi-mix of issues caused by Dad's drinking and raging and Mom's depression and hidden drug use. All of us kids festered with grief that we dare not acknowledge or express. The sticky ooze of this emotional garbage continues to spill over onto our lives as adults compelling us to clean up our own messes, take out our own trash and try to find the richness in this family compost.

I was about thirteen when suddenly our household was turned upside down. Dad lost his job due to his drinking. Mom went to work for the first time ever. Dad took us all to task to clean up the house; he ordered us around like a military drill instructor. I was shaking and quivering but I never did cry — never let him see you cry. I would march into the kitchen with my own impotent rage, slamming dishes around.

144

In my face he would yell, "Clean up this fuckin' kitchen!" He'd grab my head and push my face down onto the table if there were crumbs from breakfast and bits of last night's supper, sticky rings from glasses of juice or milk or spills that weren't cleaned up. "I want you to clean up the whole kitchen! Turn your ass around and look at this pigpen!" he'd say spinning me around. "Look at the floor! The counter! I want the whole kitchen cleaned. Jesus H Christ Almighty!!!" he'd shout with his stinky whiskey breath in my face. I wanted him to die and I wanted to die. *How can we live like this and why, why, why?*

The nuns at school would say, *God doesn't give us more than we can handle. Just dress neatly, keep your knees together girls and pray to Jesus for forgiveness and salvation.* I tried to be good but nothing worked; all that stuff —redemption and salvation— was for the other kids whose parents read them bedtime stories and tucked them in at night. I felt very alone. *What's wrong with me anyway? What's wrong with my family? Why doesn't Dad love me and why doesn't Mom get out of bed?*

No wonder now at fifty-six when I recognize I have trouble navigating the exterior world, I wonder what would healthy fathering have gotten me; I'll never know. When I start to create a healthy internal father for my little girl self, she says, "I don't need a f-ing father; I never did! I can handle it without a father!" I gently encourage her to soften, to grieve.

* * * * *

The tough bravado of my un-fathered self got me through a lot, but the kind of journey I'm on now calls for a tenderness, a softness, with the confidence and ambition of a young oak tree, strong and steady in the wind but flexible enough to bend. I didn't deserve my father's raging harshness and I don't want my internalized version of him: heavy, critical, afraid to try this or that for fear of failure or of having to do it over and over again. I am unleashing my own Great Santini to find an inner Daddy I can lean into that says, "I've got your back, honey, you can do it!"

Now as I wade through tears of grief for all that I didn't deserve, learn all that I do deserve, I think again about that garbage can next to the sink of my childhood; in my own mind I'm rummaging through it to find the ingredients, the nutrients for new green shoots, finding my version of a masculine guide, tender, young, sweet and sensitive, but also confident, excited and adventurous. He says, "I'm so sorry you experienced the harsh side of the masculine. Come with me to the softer side of the male and I will guide you."

My Dad taught me to be afraid of the world; if I don't do things right the first time I try something, then I'm stupid or there would be consequences. I want to learn something different now: to foster my own green shoots with tenderness so that I can feel more confident in the world. I want to know that whatever I do that I'm doing is right for me, that each time I try something it is a joyful experiment bringing me that much closer to what god intends for me, that my failures or early starts are a polishing of my humanity, a honing. I am a child of a divine father who thinks I am amazing and perfect just as I am.

No wonder I want to be seen and fear being seen; I wanted Dad to leave me alone, get away, stop yelling and swearing at me. I wanted him to see me as a budding young woman, to treat me as though I mattered, that I was worth knowing and recognizing. He taught me to hide from him, from the world, and from myself. The good news is I get to take out the garbage, organize new containers, maybe even start my own garden. I am that new green shoot rising up out of the compost pile, on the way to becoming a woman my father never knew but sometimes dreamed of inside his whiskey dreams where he longed for his own divine feminine.

He longed for the tenderness of his mother; she had eight children, was mentally ill and had nothing left for him. He composted his own desires in whiskey and beer; for him there were no green shoots. And so it goes from generation to generation, the garbage making no sense, green shoots going untended. And yet, I feel a beautiful perfect blossoming, sense out of nonsense, a field of blossoms awaiting me and daffodils between my toes.

This is not the end of my story but a call from the earth to dig deeper in the garden and get my hands dirty. This was never a one person story; it is generational. I see how both Dad and I suffered. How I wish some ancestors were here to ask questions to — but, no matter, their messages are written on my bones. If I dig deep enough into my very own soul I will find them there.

I wasn't always afraid of my father. I remember in my very young years looking up to him. He was six feet tall, sapphire blue eyes, wavy dark hair, very handsome with a big smile. He was gone a lot. He worked hard to provide for the family. To spend time with him was a longing never answered, like candy out of reach. "When will Dad be home?" "Later, honey." "Where is Dad?" "Working." Then when he came home he was grumpy and tired and didn't see me. He rested in his own world of worry and whiskey.

* * * * *

My Dad will soon be eighty and I still long to know him, but today that longing is partially met by pieces I have of the puzzle and by acceptance of

146

this family disease of alcoholism, the real generational monster. He was the youngest of eight on the tail end of the depression era. His father was gone a lot too; he was a traveling salesman.

As the story goes, his mother was mentally ill. I wonder about that; with eight children and a husband who was gone all the time, who wouldn't have retreated to an interior world of depression and hopelessness. Extreme poverty, no birth control, she was transported from Ireland to a land that refused her culture and kind. Her illness was at a time when patients had no rights. Her husband said she was crazy, and off she went in a paddy wagon to the nut house for months at a time.

I don't imagine anyone explained this to my Dad at age two or four. He was left a lot to fend for himself; he said he starting smoking at age four, picking butts up out of the gutter. This tells me how little parenting or supervision there was, not to mention love or tenderness. He suffered the trickle-down effects of his older brothers' rage. He was young and powerless and pissed as hell. All his needs for mothering and fathering went unmet.

Once he told me he had a dream, one that he had over and over, about a little boy outside of a big house. He was hiding along the side of it, hidden and observing from a distance. In front of the house there was a commotion, police and a wagon, and screaming and crying, and a woman taken away against her will. He dreamt this over and over until he realized he was the little boy and it was his Mom being taken away — candy always out of reach. No one to comfort him, he suffered alone. The longing for the safe soft arms of his mother is, I think, his deepest wound. In so many ways he and I have longed for the same thing: love, safety, trust, for something to count on, a tribal union.

This wound we have in common is the place to explore. I mentioned earlier that to have my longing meet his longing on some level, he would have to acknowledge his deep wound of the feminine aspect of himself. To embrace me as his precious daughter he would have to travel his own vein of gold to his un-mothered self, discover his mistrust of the feminine and his rage at her unconscious abandonment of him. I feel how painful and baffling it is to reach through my own wounds of the masculine; I avoided this my whole life, leading to incapacitation, fear of success and fear of my own power in the world. Dad mentioned to me a couple of times over the years his fear of going crazy. If he became too vulnerable, too soft, the world would take advantage of him and wreak havoc with his mind. Crazy always waiting for him; he would become his Mom, what he longed for and feared the most.

I have feared my own power and success, getting things right or wrong. If I demanded things or aggressively sought them out, I would become my Dad, a raging monster of self-will, a force to be reckoned with, a bitch, the female; the very thing Dad longed for and was terrified of. The very thing I knew I shouldn't be. Always amazes me that a man who is dominant, self advocating, aggressive, successful is called a go-getter. A woman of the same qualities is called a selfish bitch. In the house I lived in it was better to be male, the preferred gender.

* * * * *

So I want to take a look at the kitchen incident through my Dad's eyes if I can. I was laid off from work; "too much drinking" they said. What the fuck do they know! They'll give me ninety days to get sober. There's a chapter at work that helps get people into AA, as if I need it, none of their business anyway. Now I have to look good for ninety days to get my job back. Well, maybe I do have a problem and maybe I don't.

Now I'm at home and my wife has gone to work for the first time, days at Howard Johnsons. Now all the neighbors will see I'm off like some husband whose wife has to take care of him. What am I supposed to do — cook and clean? I don't think so, but I am going to get those lazy ass kids to clean up around here instead of them sleeping half the day.

My wife can't keep this place clean; we'll see what's so hard about it. I want Chris to start in the kitchen, that pigpen of a kitchen. It's always covered in garbage and crap spilled everywhere, sticky floors. I fuckin' go to work all day and I don't know what anyone else does around this place. My wife thinks she can sleep half the day and not do shit. Well, that's over for now! Now that she's got the job, I'm at home now and she'll see what it's like to go to work all day. I'll show her how to run a house the way it should be run.

I need a drink real bad. I feel sick and my hands are shaky. I'm sweating all over and I vomited a couple of times this morning, a retching all the way down to my toes. I'm trying really hard not to drink. Gotta go to those meetings and get my job back. I've got a headache and I feel a rage at the world, at everyone. I don't really think I have a problem but my boss thinks I do. That bitch of a wife wouldn't even cover for me and now the boss knows I couldn't make it because of a couple of drinks. I'm going to put my energy into the house and the kids today when I get home.

"Chris, I want you to clean this god-forsaken kitchen; show your mother how it's really done. I want it clean! I don't care if the sink is stopped up; I don't want any excuses. Just clean it!" Stupid girl is just like her mother. Chris is starting to get upset but I don't really care. I want a drink, just one and I will be okay. I don't know why I'm shaking so badly.

Part of me feels good yelling at Chris; can't stand whining, crying women. I feel a sense of power. I am the man of the house. I am the father. I'm supposed to be in charge here. But I also see out of the corner of my awareness that I'm swearing at her, raging at her way beyond the situation. So what, she'll get over it and I wouldn't be raging if everyone did what they were supposed to do and get off my back, especially if I could have a few drinks. I know she sides with her mother and thinks I have a problem too, even though she hasn't said so. I can see it in her eyes: the fear, the blame, the hurt. But I can't deal with that. I just keep hammering her down with my large, loud self. I don't have to deal with that other stuff.

She cleans the kitchen but does such a half ass job. She did the dishes and wiped around the sink, but the garbage is still there and the table and floor are a mess. Who is she kidding? When I look at the mess, a rage so huge builds up in me. I trigger off and grab Chris and shove her face into the table. Even as I do it I can't believe I'm doing it. I want someone to see, someone to be accountable, someone to be responsible for all this besides me.

I tell her she is good for nothing, can't do anything right. Can't clean the kitchen, its so simple. I don't understand why she can't get it right. Can't do what I tell her to. She starts to quiver under my hands and I feel a wave of shame. How can I do this, she's my daughter? Why do I always hurt the ones I love? If I just had one drink I would be better. I'm a better person when I drink, more even-keeled. Everything seems easier.

But I can't, so all I have is this rage and I can't help it. I shove her across the kitchen. So what. She doesn't cry. She never cries, a tough girl, a chip off the old block. I tell her to clean it again and again. Clean it one hundred times until its right. She turns her back on me and starts again to do what I asked her to. Just for a second I wonder why I rage at her and her Mom. What is it about women that drive me insane? They are pretty and soft and tender but I don't trust them. They are only good for one thing; otherwise they are a pain in the ass. They call on some part of my heart that is broken, abandoned, cast away; too dangerous to go near. God I need a drink!

* * * * *

My Dad and I have something in common in that kitchen incident, one of hundreds like it. He needs his whiskey river and I don't really care. I want him to have his booze and get out of my face. Even at the age of thirteen I can see he is sick; I can feel every cell of his body needs that drink. Sooner or later the aching chemistry of it all will wear him down. A part of me wants to reach out to him, tell him I love him, but the monster prevails and it's not safe. He wants to leave me alone and go drink and I want him to leave me alone and go get drunk or something. Perhaps my fear and disgust even give him permission, and his guilt and shame win the drink every time.

149

I'm not sure what is the main tragedy here — that he is an alcoholic, or that I am the abused child? Or that he is the abused and abandoned one from his childhood and only dishes up what he knows? Certainly these are all great sorrows. But most of all the tragedy is this: that as my father approaches his eightieth birthday I have not known him. He has not known me. When I have not known my father, how much harder it is to know myself? I only knew him as monster, larger than life, a whiskey-scented deranged man. I can see his five-year-old self, afraid of the world, puffed up with hot air, but I did not know that little boy and he did not know me.

I am fifty-seven and ours is the longest relationship I have and we do not know each other authentically in any way. We had the opportunity to be father and daughter, friends, members of the same tribe, but we were not. It is not that we failed at love. Alcoholism robbed us of much of our humanity, our ordinariness. I imagine that ordinariness is a necessary factor in the father-daughter relationship: pancakes made on a lazy Sunday morning together, learning to dance by standing on his shoes and having him waltz me around the living room, treating me as though I was his princess. These are memories I do not have.

This is the bottom of my grief—to have missed out on knowing another human being, to watch him age and begin that long journey to the other world while part of me screams, "Wait! Wait! Who are you and why can't we do this the right way?" As if this was the end of the story. But it is not the end; it is the beginning of my knowing myself and the internalized version of my Dad...the monster within.

Making peace with him/me and developing the best internal Daddy I can. I would like to think that when my Dad passes over he will cheer me on from afar, finally able to tap into love and send me blessings. The abused child is never without hope. I can hope that death will heal him into love and that on some plane our spirits will meet and know each other completely. I accept now that this was the life we had. A life detoured by the disease of addiction, the stealer of love. This was my greatest pain and my greatest gift because it sent me on a journey of self-love, compassion and forgiveness. These things will always be a journey for me and not a destination.

Most of all I know that in that kitchen there was a millisecond of love where I saw his disease and wished it were different, and he knew he was abusing me and wishes he wasn't. And then that second is gone. Poof! Gone but never forgotten. A millisecond of love is not enough but when it's all there is, it's important to acknowledge it.

We were all so very sick but not without love. Moments of love and a lifetime of sorrow. I wish I had a happy ending here to tie it all up nicely, but life has its own way of telling the story. I could reach up that vein of gold and express tenderness to my father. But, I have done my time on Maple Dr. and I won't put myself in the line of fire again.

My father came to visit me recently. I had hoped for something different but he brought his barbed-wire heart with him, along with his disrespect of women and his ever-present addiction. I saw him in a new light as a man who has built walls around to protect himself and to keep people out. I respected his walls and didn't feel I needed to scale them or remove them, as if I could. But occasionally his guard would drop and there would be a kind of raw and indirect love. Love nonetheless. It was my birthday and he asked me what I wanted. I gave him some options and he elected to buy me perfume.

I have always loved fragrance and now I know why. In our house with the sheet rock falling down and the police coming frequently we had the best bouquets of flower fresh-cut from around the yard. One spray of perfume and I am surrounded by the beauty my father created, his garden of roses and lilacs, the greenness of spring in the warmth of the sun. There is no one who has an eye for flowers who is without a heart for love, including my father. As for me, thanks to this negative teaching, I have a tender heart and a huge capacity for love.

Raud Kennedy

Making My Own Acquaintance

I used to smoke, crave it, enjoy it.
Now it's something people do
who are ambivalent about life,
not sure if they want to live or die.
I used to drink a lot.
It was the high and low of my day.
Now it's what people do who are in pain.
Their pain has taken on a life of its own
and needs to be fed and cared for
like a lost soul they've brought home from the bar.
I used to feel sad and needed that sadness
to have something to escape from
because without it I'd be left alone
experiencing an uncomfortable silence
with a stranger.

Meeting My Past

Some insights are so clear to me today
that I accept them as truths.
But only a few years ago
I would've been hesitant
to consider them at all.
If I met my old self on the street
and we talked over a meal,
I'd consider him problematic
and be concerned for his future.
I'd have no desire to be pals
and would walk away after our meal,
relieved to be free of him,
and he'd probably feel the same.
His addictions would make him uneasy.
My sobriety would remind him
of the demons nipping at his heels
that he would soon have to face.
But he'd come up with another reason
to avoid that thought.
He'd say to himself,
that guy is quiet, that guy is dull,
and his impatience to lift his next drink
would write me off.

Ann Mintz

A Fate Worse than Death

That's what it used to be called but I can say with absolute authority that it's not. Don't get me wrong, there's nothing good about rape. When someone steps that far over the line, you have no way of knowing how far he is going to go. After it happens to you, for a while, maybe for a very long while, it's all you can think about. But you can get over being raped. You can't get over being dead.

Russ Allison Loar

My Father Among the Chinese

The Chinese children watched the funny fat American in the ridiculous sport coat try to blow up the balloons.

He was a tourist in his late 60s, wearing a gray floppy hat. His face was a fleshy sagging caricature of itself, accented by an unkempt bushy salt-and-pepper mustache intended to disguise the steady loss of masculinity from his features.

Someone back home had told him that Chinese children love balloons. But what really caught the attention of the children was the exuberant vaudeville of this short-winded, red-faced man in the funny clothing who was having an extraordinarily difficult time inflating the balloons which were too small and thin for such an amateur. Each balloon he attempted to inflate flew from his lips into the air with the sound of a small fart, prompting laughter and applause from the children gathered around him.

My father, a man who once made deals with some of the most influential businessmen in America, had successfully transformed himself into an amusing street monkey.

Later that day he would show a group of Chinese university students how to peel an orange.

CRUXES

Yu-Han Chao

Why I Did Not Become a World-Famous Classical Violinist

There were many reasons I did not become a world-famous classical violinist. So many things were in the way—so many distractions, disappointments, mean and scary people...

Here are my excuses:

1. I Was Too Short.

My evil violin teacher said this when I was fifteen:
"You're too short to play the violin."
I already had an inferiority complex about my height and never hung out with tall people. What she said did not help. It was one more thing on the list of privileges my shortness denied me.

List of things I can't do because I'm short:
   a. Wear long dresses (a fashion advisor on the radio said so)
   b. Wear my hair too long (everybody says this; it makes you look even shorter)
   c. Become a stewardess, a strangely glamorous job where I come from (you have to be at least 160 centimeters)
   d. Become a model (you have to be 168 centimeters)
   e. Go out with tall men (I hate them because I'm short)
   f. Reach the two higher shelves of my cabinets
   g. Play the violin

2. I Did Not Have the Rack

Have you ever seen Ann-Sophie Mutter in concert? She wears these beautiful low cut strapless evening dresses. I do not have the rack to hold up such a dress. Even if I held it up momentarily, with a few larger movements of the bow and after some especially vigorous four-string chords, my low cut strapless evening dress a la Mutter would without doubt slide straight to the floor. This happened to one of my mom's friends once. People have no sympathy in these situations.

As a pre-adolescent, I heard an awful rumor about playing violins and violas—it makes one of your breasts bigger/smaller than the other. It was because of where the instrument pressed down—it squeezed the meat down and either stimulated or stunted growth on one side of one's

158

budding chest. This made me even less enthusiastic about practicing. Sometimes I played the violin with opposite arms and hands, hoping to counter the damage my musical education was possibly doing to my already underdeveloped figure. So I held the neck of the violin in my right hand and sawed at the strings with the left, ignoring the fact that I was missing the chin rest entirely, there was much pain, and I couldn't make anything but chicken-slaughtering noises. At least both of my tits would be the same size.

3. I Had Some Really Mean Teachers

All of the violins I used before I got my current second full-sized violin were stained with tears. The tears made ugly marks, like those left on black pants after one walks in week-old snow. The edges were squiggly, white, looked almost crusty, and were salty if you licked them out of curiosity. I cried because quite a few of my teachers were nasty, nasty people, whom I suspected enjoyed tormenting me and making me sob.

My first teacher, Mr. Bregazzo in California, was the only nice teacher I had. Even so, I cried more than once or twice in his music room during the four or five years I studied with him since kindergarten. He would take out this little mechanism filled with water, and show me little blue beads of liquid which slid down several slides, wheels, and landed a the bottom of the hour-glass like cylindrical container.

"Look, it's crying too." He would say.

Mr. Bregazzo was well into his 70s when I went to him for classes, and whenever my dad left the room I would secretly panic—what would I do if Mr. Bregazzo croaked in the middle of the lesson? Should I run for help? Yell out the window? Look for his wife downstairs in the kitchen, his wife Nancy whom I'd never spoken to?

I haven't seen Mr. Bregazzo for over ten years; he's still living, and the last time my mom went to see him, he was all alone in his big house in Orange County and he had lost his wife and part of his mind. He asked my mom to marry him. I wouldn't have liked to be there to witness that; I liked Mr. Bregazzo too much.

My next violin teacher was originally a viola player, and she only taught violin to make more money at our music school. She scolded me, yelled, had no patience whatsoever, and was married to a hairy biologist she didn't seem to like. They translated a book about apes together, and the harder she worked on her project, the less sleep she had, the more she screamed at me to make me cry. I would try the best I could to continue

159

playing though crying made me tremble, which made the sounds coming out of my violin slippery and staccatoed, which further incensed her.

Then there was the teacher I had in high school who was the one who announced that I was too short to play the violin in the first place. She sold my mom expensive used bows and made me take a lot of extra lessons. Even when I played extremely well at a violin exam, she still wasn't happy. She also told one of my fellow students that his fingers were too deformed to play the violin.

She was pretty, however, beautiful in a masculine way. She had short cropped hair and wore sunglasses and form-fitting, creased pants. When she walked into our school, trendy Ray-Ban shades gleaming, short hair bouncing, holding her large rectangular violin case, standing at her full height of maybe 165 centimeters, I thought she was the coolest violin-playing woman on earth. She would lower her sunglasses and ask my classmates where the hell I was, it was time for my lesson, and they would call my name up the hallway and stairs. My classmates would admire her lavender-blue eye shadow and later come to me and say: "Your violin teacher is so beautiful and so ku, cool and handsome as a man."

I had a love-hate relationship with that ku woman. I wanted to be her but she kept shooting me down so I resented her at the same time that I idolized her. I went to all of her performances, brought flowers and clapped loudly, spoke well of her to the parents of her other violin students, all the time that she continued stepping all over me, causing me pain...

4. Music School Was a Screwy Place

Music school was not just a home to mean teachers, it was also the home of screwed up kids. Imagine a group of children who had known one another all of their lives, who had competed against one another at intense competitions and been envious of one another for more than ten years beginning from childhood. The violin and viola players with calloused fingers and scars on their necks, the flute players with lips that stuck out like goldfish, harp players with bandaged fingers, tuba and trumpet players had mouths that always looked like they just swallowed an egg—this was a collection of warped people indeed.

I learned not to trust my "friends" in music school. They saved notes you passed to them in class and later used them against you in the strangest situations. They stole money. They were selfish; they spared no one.

160

One moment of truth for me was during a bi-monthly violin exam. The judges sat inside a large music room, and we examinees went in one by one. One of the walls of the music room was just a huge pane of glass adjacent to the hallway, so we could all see what was going on inside, see every frown on the judges' faces as our fellow students played. At the time, one girl, Sun, a rather plump but muscular and strong violin major who had a great stage presence and usually did well, forgot her score and stopped. On the other side of the glass, in the hallway, I saw the other violin majors smile and grin at one another, gratified. I could not believe that they were so happy at someone else's failure, and expressing it so blatantly, as a group. Sun was a nice girl. I was a violin major, too. When it was my turn to enter the room full of judges, I could still see the gratified grins of my classmates, and could feel them hoping I would fall on my face, too.

5. My Brother

Now, my brothers are old enough to be subjected to a musical education as well, but before that, my youngest brother used to cover his ears whenever I played the violin and yell over my playing, "It's too much noise! Too much noise! Let me *diiiiie*! I'm dying of the noise—"
My mom would rush over to shut him up but I was already angry beyond words, ready to hit him, tears stinging my eyes, which were nearsighted from reading too many microscopic scores and blurry with fatigue. As if I didn't hate having to play enough already, damn kid...

I was vindicated, however, when a few years later, my mom broke a violin bow in half hitting that same bigmouthed brother.

6. Computer Games

My brothers shared with me innumerable computer games on which I could waste my life. We played Tetris, Chinese Chess, Pinball, and many other games, but the most addictive of all were Role-Playing Games (RPG) where monkey-like animated figures scurried about the screen fighting monsters and enemies. The RPGs were addictive because they never had to end, you could just keep killing enemies and earning points and becoming more powerful—have more blood, better weapons, better animals to ride, etc. In some cases you could mutate from a simple soldier to a general on a horse to a bigger general on a flying horse to a warrior queen on a flying dragon. It was the most exciting thing ever for me.

I spent a lot of time on these games instead of playing the violin. In fact, for most of my years in music school, I rarely practiced. Before my

161

mom left the house, I would pick up my violin and play a few tentative notes. Sometimes I played a little longer so that she could hear me from the street as she got into a taxi. But by the time she was far, far away from hearing distance I would flip the score to the last page, indicating that I had played the piece to the end (for mom to see when she came home), drop my violin and bow on the sofa and plop down before my computer to slaughter some more beasts or make my way into the nearly impossible Tetris high score list.

7. The Disharmony Between Mother and Me

I didn't like my mom very much as a child. She wanted too much for me to become a world-famous classical violinist. Once when I was in first grade I remembered my dad asking my mom a question, "What exactly do you intend her to become after all this?"

Mom: "I want her to be a genius."

Me: Silent in the back seat, freaked out. Note that my mother conveniently did not understand the true meaning of the word "genius"—that you are born that way. Sure, I had perfect pitch, quick fingers, but I was horrified of my mother and did not want to play the violin or become a violinist or violin teacher. I did not want to give her that satisfaction.

As I grew older, my mother and I had many more fights over music. She said that she never had the chance to study music as a child, that her father was against it, and now that I had access to everything she didn't have, I had better darn well be grateful, work hard, and cherish my opportunities. But after one final fight, I left music school, went to a private school where I was beaten so badly by teachers that my hands were all bruised black and blue but I didn't tell anyone at home. Eventually, I got into a great university and my mom stopped saying music was the only thing I could do.

8. I Was More Interested in Martial Arts

Before I got into university, I had secretly read shelves-full of martial arts novels and some real martial arts instruction books. I studied and practiced the Praying Mantis Quan extensively, and dabbled in a few other schools of Quan (fist). Once I jumped up and kicked a wall so hard I busted my ankle and couldn't go to school the next day. I lied about why I had hurt myself because I couldn't tell anyone that I was practicing my flying kick and had misjudged the hardness of the wall.

In university, I got to take some Judo, Sing-i Quan, and Chi Gon in various PE classes. I wanted to see myself as one of those people in flowing robes in martial arts novels, who flew from tree to tree, fought skillfully, was so quick it seemed I had multiple arms and legs, and could assassinate evil men with secret weapons like poisoned flying needles and spiked discs.

9. I Was More Interested in Gymnastics

I was part of the gymnastics club in university. I practiced two times a week for hours, now that I had lots of free time left over from not playing the violin or piano. We even went to a tournament in Tai Chong and won fourth place in the amateur competition (there were only four groups in the competition, but nobody has to know that). I could work the balance beam, parallel bars, and could do almost every trick imaginable on the large spring bed. Now that I think of it, I could have killed myself by landing on my neck from a back flip, but when you're younger you don't think about such things.

10. I Got Accepted to the English Department

Being at a good university gave me lots of confidence to be whatever I wanted to be in the future (that was not violin-related) and the English Department showed me literature, writing, and a nice sort of academic escapism. I read so much that finally, I had to write too. I went to England, Ireland, and saw how large the world was, how nice people could be—not everyone was a music school teacher or music school student. And not everyone in music was evil, I later found. Although one of my mom's professor friends in America claimed that all musicians were bisexual, or wanted to be, if they had the chance.

I did eventually teach some classical violin, but not in a music school, and I was a very nice instructor/tutor who never minded if a student obviously hadn't practiced all week. These kids didn't have to become world-famous violinists because I hadn't either; there was no pressure. They could become anything they wanted, and they didn't have to learn this in a hard way.

Helen Ruggieri

Haibun

AT THE LAKE

I'd swim out to the dock floating on old oil cans at the edge of the cove. You could see the white faces of cottages set among the trees, a glimmer of beaches, bright sails on the small sailboats. A bright sun would make gold squiggles, a sort of writing on the surface of the water, a far away motor boat would send ripples rocking and slapping the raft.

Maybe a radio would be playing top forty and the favorite songs of the moment would flutter by, loud and soft and you'd try to fill in what was missing.

I'd rub myself with coconut oil and stretch out to dry on the worn warm boards, the sun beating into the flesh, a tan you could still enjoy.

I would be happy. The moment, this moment. Ashamed almost this love of aloneness. The sun cutting an edge around you.

    so quiet
    in the trees
    gypsy moths munch

BIRTH OF TIME

In Sunday school the teacher gave us a beautiful green and yellow picture of a garden. She explained that every week we came we would get a sticker to paste in the blank white spaces that appeared in the picture. I pasted in my first sticker of the boy Christ resplendent in a purple robe standing front center. I looked at all the other holes in the picture and tried to come to an understanding of how long it would take to fill in all the holes. Next week and the week after and on and on. Time was some dark endless tunnel I had to crawl through to get my picture filled in.

I kept my picture for years until it began to disintegrate from the edges inward. The beginning of time and its power over us.

blank spaces
in our recall –
my mother's face

DEER RUN

At twilight the deer drift down to the long fields to feed when the snow has drifted deep in the hollows between the long chain of rounded hills. The barren hardwoods make a gray haze in the winter light and as the valley floor begins to rise there are hemlock and pine. Deer walk a random narrow path to the meadow, stamp glyphs in the snow where they graze and drift away into the early dark.

I bring essentials – stove, chair, table, a window facing the field. Days are short, nights, long; and when a tree falls, there is no sound.

> December dusk
> a solitary pine tree
> all lit up

FALLING ASLEEP

I want to go to sleep but I can't. To fall asleep I have to have a piece of silk, the binding on a blanket to hold on to as I drop off into darkness.

I had rubbed all the silk off the binding. My mother turned the blanket around to find a small tatter of silk for me to hang on to so I could fall away into night.

> the night is dark
> and long and you might die
> before you wake

FRENCH ASYLUM

We drove to the crematorium in the gray Scranton morning. My mother cried for her baby brother, Uncle Sandy, and a childhood that we knew nothing of.

She refused to leave him there alone, wanting to stay until the fire consumed his earthly body, but the pastor told her Sandy wasn't alone now, he'd found peace.

Our duty done, we turned home along Route 6 until a detour took us down from the mountain side into a dense green Susquehanna valley and I saw a sign – French Asylum, 2 miles – and begged to go.

We turned down a rutted road with weeds scraping the bottom of the car to see pasture going back to pine like everywhere else and not the grand mansion exiled aristocrats had prepared for Marie Antoinette when she was rescued from the French revolutionaries.

I hid my disappointment at the loss of what had seemed so real to me. But my sister wouldn't let it go. She yelled at me for being so dumb, and my father yelled at her for yelling at me, and my mother yelled at all of us for yelling with Sandy new dead, and we drove on in silence.

The sun hung low over the hills and all that green expanse speeding by glowed with a brilliance that made my eyes water. It was an alchemical change, the green turned into gold, dissolving the usual, the ordinary, transforming it into something that never tarnishes no matter how long it's buried under the sun.

> purple clover
> catches twilight at the
> bottom of the field

Linda Mussillo

Ordering

The waitress approached our table tentatively; I could see it in her eyes, read her mouth, almost twitching before she spoke. She took my order first, and then it came:

"...What does he want?"

It hadn't been the first time. She was young for a waitress, but I was younger – maybe ten; it was no excuse.

I picked up my fallen stomach and did the thing I hadn't done before.

"Why don't you ask him?" My voice rang.

My blind father relaxed his posture and smiled by inches even though he couldn't see the red rise up in her face.

Cari Oleskewicz

Notes for My Therapist

Okay, doctor, you are a professional and I am a pragmatist and we don't have a lot of time together, particularly at the first session. The first therapy session is always awkward because we don't know how the other works, thinks, reacts, and so there's this hesitancy on both our parts. Right? I would like to avoid all that by giving you an outline which will give you some background information on my yet-undiagnosed mental illness(es) and offer you a glimpse of what you have coming next Tuesday at 5:45 pm. We'll be able to hit the ground running and dive into whatever it is you think is wrong with me, tell me how to fix it, and if necessary, prescribe the applicable medication.

A. My family. I don't even know where to start. I am the eldest of four, the responsible one, the caretaker and babysitter, the one who didn't fit in with her parents or her sisters, who kind of dangled there in the Purgatory of the family unit. I feel intense pain every time one of my parents or sisters is hurting and I feel responsible for fixing every aspect of their lives that brings them discomfort. I want them never to feel badly. Will I be this way raising my own child? Because I know feeling badly and failing are part of growing, I know that intellectually, but if anyone hurts my child or causes her to cry, I swear to God I will unleash a wrath upon them that may show up on the national security radar. Anyway, I am preoccupied with the feelings of my family members. It's stressful. When two or more of them are fighting with each other, I binge on junk food and begin to have heart palpitations. I become paranoid that it's my fault. I'll also want to explore my relationships with each of my sisters. I'm closest with the youngest one, and I feel guilty about that when it comes to the second one. The third one is a little nuts and she is also the favorite of my mother, so there are a host of issues there. When I say she's a little nuts I mean that she makes shit up, including relationships, and she has a history of stalking people. A total psycho. But I love and feel responsible for her too. There are also lots of secrets in my family. I'm not sure if I want to discover them, if that would help me, or if it would only make me need something more than your services, something like an inpatient program.

B. Divorce. Yes, I've been separated for about 9 months and our divorce will be final in the next few weeks. I never should have married this guy. He's a total doormat and never challenged me in any way. I'm pretty sure I never loved him. I mean, I love him as I love all humanity, but there was never any marital love. It felt like I was his mother rather than his wife. He wouldn't so much as buy milk when we ran out without calling to check with me first. Maddening. He was also afraid of the telephone – would not even call to order a pizza. I knew going into the marriage that it was wrong, but the Bishop had already been booked and my mother had already done the seating arrangements and I have a big problem disappointing people, so we went ahead with it and four years later it's a complete disaster and he's broken-hearted and always looking at me either like he's about to cry or chop me into a million pieces and bury me in my tomato garden, which is now just a pile of brown, crispy leaves and slimy bugs. I worry about the effect of the divorce on my daughter and I wonder what people think of me. This one jackass I work with, the I.T. guy who everyone hates, offered me his condolences and said, "let me guess – he left you for a woman half your size?" What the hell kind of thing is that to say to someone? I immediately ate a bag of candy and cried for three days.

C. Eating. I have food issues. This comes from my childhood, I am sure. I was a competitive gymnast and I've been called fat since I was eight years old. I have no rational concept of what is fat and what is thin because when I was thirteen and weighed 102 pounds, I was told I had to lose at least ten pounds to stay on the gymnastics team. My mother used to call me Crisco (fat in the can). All of my sisters have weight issues too, as do my aunts on my mother's side. My mother, however, is thin. What kind of mental torture is that? I'm also obsessed with food, particularly candy. On my lunch hour last week I bought a bag of Reese's Pieces – the big 16-ounce bag. I left the bag in the car so I wouldn't eat the whole thing during my afternoon at work, but I found myself thinking about that candy the entire rest of the day. I planned for it. I envisioned opening the trunk and getting out the bag so I could eat it while I drove home. I imagined the comfort of finishing it off in front of Law & Order reruns on television that night, after I put my daughter to bed. I could not focus on any of my work. If I obsessed like that over a controlled substance or a bottle of alcohol, someone would help me. And don't tell me to eat less and exercise more, or I will take a swing at you. It doesn't work like that for me. Crisco has to eat all of the chips in a bag, all of the ice cream in a tub, and then feel sick about it later.

171

D. Chores. I am unable to do the mundane things in life that everyone else seems to do without complaint or drama. I cannot cope with making lunch for my daughter. Extracting two pieces of whole grain bread from the bag, unscrewing the cap on the peanut butter and bending into the refrigerator for the jelly are all actions that I dread, so I don't do it the night before like I should – I end up doing it when we should have left the house 10 minutes ago, which only makes the chore a hundred times more disgusting to me. The handle on the knife I use inevitably becomes sticky and this makes me want to cry. I also cannot cope with sweeping the floor or hand-washing the stock pot I used to make pasta four nights ago. Is it just laziness, or something more troublesome?

E. Running. I have a constant desire to move. Right now I cannot stand this town that I live in, particularly the way no one here speaks proper English and thinks the "to be" verb is optional. If I hear one more person say "the car needs washed," I may lose my mind. I need to be back in a city, where there is intellectualism and movies with subtitles and good Asian food. But then when I'm in the city, I crave the country, where I can feel superior to everyone because I'm from the city. I usually stay in a place a maximum of two years and then I'm on the move. It used to feel therapeutic to me to rip my life apart every couple of years and start over. But now I have a child to think about, who would probably benefit from some semblance of stability. And it would be nice to make some friends and put down roots and get involved in the community and all that. So how come I don't want to? And by the way, I'm not good at making friends. People irritate me, especially the people I like. It's like I'm never satisfied or something.

F. Anxiety. This is the real reason I need medication – I have actual visions of my heart popping through my chest cavity, out of my body and on to my lap. Sometimes I get all worked up, either because someone has upset me, or I'm remembering the terribly uncomfortable hugs my Uncle Pete used to give me, or I'm thinking about making my daughter's sandwich and wondering whether she has eaten a vegetable all week, or I'm worried that my mother knows how much I resent my sisters, or I'm terrified my dad's feelings have been hurt by something I've said or done or haven't said or haven't done, or I'm in a meeting with the directors and I start to think about my to-do list, and I can honestly feel my heart begin to beat faster and faster and closer to my skin. Or, what if it happens in the night and my daughter wakes up to find me non-responsive on my bed because of my heart explosion and she doesn't know what to do? When will someone come? And what if she wanders around the house and grabs a butcher knife or starts a fire? Dear God, it's happening right now, that light-headed chest thumping feeling and I can actually imagine the organ beating on the outside of my body, flushed and tired, and then just giving up. This cannot be normal.

So, there you have it. At least, it's all I can think of for right now. Better to get this off to you right away so I can't spend anymore time on it. I want to save something for therapy, right?

I look forward to seeing you next Tuesday.

Carmen Anthony Fiore

Open Letter to My Dead Mother

Okay, Mom, I know you've been gone for twenty-four years, but I still want to get a few things off my mind (or out of my spleen, would be a better way to put it), before I take the "swan dive" into eternity's black hole.

1. Why did you always compare me to your first-born son (your favorite), whom you and Pop put up on a pedestal, turning the bastard into the family's conceited elitist snob? He became a legend in his own mind and ended up believing his own bullshit.

2. Remember when I brought you up to my new home in the woodsy countryside of Hunterdon County, New Jersey, and the first words out of your mouth (as you stood in the expansive foyer) were, "Ernie should have this house," and afterwards you never said anything else about the house, never even wished me and Catherine "the best of luck with your beautiful new house" or anything else complimentary?

3. And I can't forget when you were dying by degrees in a Trenton, New Jersey, hospital, and I dutifully visited you. But you told your nurse, "My son Ernie was here to see me." Well, I've got news for you, Mom, Ernie never visited you at the hospital. He only came to Trenton when he needed to borrow money off you and Pop and never paid a dime of it back. When I found that out, it was like another dagger got well-placed into my heart: I do the visit, he gets the credit.

Hope you can rest in peace, Mom, because I don't think I'll be able to enjoy eternity, knowing I was always an afterthought in your eyes.

Your invisible son, the writer?

Carmen Anthony Fiore

174

Amber L. West

Untitled

Recently, I came across pictures I took of my breasts in the mirror with my cell phone before my double mastectomy a few months ago. As I accidentally came across those images, I remembered that when I took them I thought I would be upset the first time I saw them after the surgery. I wasn't.

Ever since the surgery, I see my breasts quite often in my mind's eye. Often they're just in the back of my mind but sometimes I think about them. When I am remembering my hands on my breasts, touching them protectively as I did before the surgery, it almost feels as if I am really touching them.

It surprised me at first that I didn't find it difficult to see the images of my breasts looking back at me from my cell phone. But then I realized that I will remember my breasts forever – they're with me always, no pictures necessary. They live in my memory. Their absence, coupled with a ghost like reminiscence, is starting to become a part of who I am.

After a mastectomy, there is some numbness. If my arm brushes lightly across my chest, it can feel as if it's not my body I'm brushing into. That bothers me. But as significant as the numbness is, so also is my gratitude – I don't have cancer in my body anymore. I feel a huge relief about that. And then, inevitably, sadness follows. It's heavy, sweet and wistful, like for an old lover. You know the kind – the one you couldn't be with, the one you just had to let get away.

Catherine Lee

East Coast

Back East, in that melting pot of dreams,
I was raised in the Virginia fray with the
B-boys,
Skaters,
Surfers,
And don't forget the Squids
With their crew cuts, or the
Rednecks,
Ballers,
Beach
Bums with their toes in hot Carolina sand.
That's how I knew that I was just a speck.

        I was like a green shoot
      In red Georgia clay,
    Learning to
  Love,
Pray,
Hate,
Hurt,
Fear,
Win,
Weep,
  Hope,
    The hard way,
      Always the hard way.
        Hard like a cold Philly night.

Robert F. Reid-Pharr

The Cleaning Man's Son

She sat there posing, sturdy thin brown-skinned body in crinoline and curls, propped on top of a plastic covered sofa in a favorite aunt's house, pouty and cute as a rented photographer captured her pretty sepia image within the heavy void of a mounted camera. The boy recalls that day, the day of his first real memory, whenever he feels lost, whenever he finds himself in need of some soothingly pleasant anchor. He can almost hear the timbre of his many aunts' heavy cooing, their quiet laughter as they shoo their children into and out of the photographer's dull gaze, all the while primping slick/straightened hair and buttoning Sunday/shiny suits. The children so lovely, so delicious in their white dresses and blue trousers, their legs dangling from the unvanquished plastic slip cover, so amusing and provocative. Theirs was a cotton-candy sweet brown family come together to pay an expensive pink photographer so that they might share a fresh afternoon of sober recollection, a lifetime of remembering.

Later the boy's mother and aunts will insist that he could not possibly recall this day. They will say that he was far too young to know what was happening. That's why there was no picture of him. He couldn't have been counted on to sit stiff and alert while the photographer made his long exposures.

Still, the boy sees that day as clear as any. The bright late summer light streaming through windows framed by stained glass. Finger sandwiches and deviled eggs keeping him busy and content as eight heavy-thighed sisters herded surprisingly well-behaved offspring into the world of respectable image-making. Happy and fun, vivid and clean. The boy standing in the kitchen, his nose just barely running while his sister mounted the white couch like an anxious queen. Him not a bit jealous, seeing everything from where he was standing, eating deviled eggs and having his head pressed nonchalantly against this heavy thigh and that while his sister and cousins sat deathly still in the immaculate rigidity of the living room's soft light.

But that is an old memory. So old, in fact, that the boy has come to doubt it himself. It was so long ago. Perhaps his aunts were right after all. Maybe this is just some perfect story he tells himself about a perfectly-framed picture that still hangs just slightly askew in the hallway of a two-story suburban home. What he describes now might just be some well-worked narrative with which he protects himself from the damp and boredom of particularly rainy Wednesdays. Best to be certain; better to begin with something of which he is absolutely sure, something that he knows that he knows. The truth, handed down from generation to generation like some pint-sized gospel.

Charlotte. 1970. Summer.

"Pooky wake up!" His sister's face pressed close to his, sweaty and tired, too old for a little girl, too afraid and urgent. She needed him then. Her nerves had gotten the best of her. She needed to go to the bathroom, needed to release her anxiety in a heavy yellow stream splashing hard and complaining against molded porcelain. Mama and Daddy were fighting and since there was no one better to take her place, her little brother would just have to do. Better to snatch him from a deep sleep than to find herself, a half-grown girl of ten, with pee running down her leg while she stood between arguing Titans, trying to get Mama not to provoke Daddy too bad, trying to get Daddy to stay at home, trying with all her little girl whiles to convince her parents to sit down for whiskey, Coca Cola, recrimination, and glum resignation, to turn their ugly attentions toward their hysterical child instead of their own vulgar histrionics.

She needed the boy to come, heavy in his bedclothes. She needed him to just stand there, to act as a fleshy, undersized barrier, not much use in a real storm but perhaps strong enough to temporarily keep the girl's dangerously young parents from the viciousness of their own immaturity, the savagery of their unacknowledged fears. He would be her sentry, the peacemaker who might keep Mama's curses from turning to slaps and Daddy's plaintive drawls from congealing into solid punches. Another black eye? Mama could handle it, but the girl could not. How did you explain such things to the neighbors? Worse yet, how did you avoid explaining it? How did you go out the next day to ride bikes or play in the creek knowing that they knew, that they'd heard near as much as you had, that your family's roaring shame was served up like butter heavy popcorn in some Saturday night movie house?

That's what was wrong. None of them knew when to stop. They always allowed their drama to tarry overlong; Mama and Daddy, the boy and Shacky, in the driveway, on the back lawn, their business all in the street. Daddy edging into his white Lincoln Continental, Mama cussing and fighting. Daddy telling her to stop raising all that sand.

The boy was no slouch though. He understood his part; knew just where to scatter into the street after Mama threw her purse at the retreating Lincoln, knew where to pick up the lipsticks and the cigarettes, not bothering himself about the way Mama cussed and cried herself back into the house, cussing more than crying. In truth, Mama rarely cried. Or better put, when the stray tear did slip quick and hot down her cheek, she was mostly far too embarrassed of herself to allow things to go much further than that, to let loose all the ugly hurting and wanting that kept her wound so tight, so hot, so sweet, so mean, needy all at the same time.

Yes, Mama could cuss. Still, she never really seemed to let go of herself. The boy only saw that once or twice. Her on the floor, Daddy in a rage, her night dress up around her hips, Daddy planting a solid kick in her stomach before he retreated to the tranquility of F.M. radio and fake leather. Mama on the side of a country grave, thigh-thick sisters to her right and left, wailing about how she was an orphan now, her own daddy and mama both buried in country graves.

And though no one ever seemed to notice, the boy would never have thought to mention that he'd seen anything like that. Even though people always accused him of carrying tales and staying in grown folks' business, he had learned early —early and well— how to keep his mouth shut, how to act dumb, though dumb he most certainly was not, how to pretend that he'd not heard nothing in Mama's cussing about other women or outside children, in daddy's about a man's needs or a wife's coldness.

Besides, his bitter, fragile little family needed his strangely calm retreat back into the house after it was all over, the nonchalance of his climb back into his bed, or the sweat-soaked bed of his trembling, angry sister. They all needed his forgetfulness, the way he'd eat whatever Mama cooked the next day for breakfast, and laugh with painful glee as Daddy pushed him high, too high, in the swing. They needed him to scamper, thighs as thick as any of his aunts, onto the white seats of the Lincoln when miraculously Mama and Daddy decided that bygones were gone by, that it was time for fried chicken, Hush Puppies, and a fun family trip to the drive-in movies. Buck and the Preacher, Cooley High, the boy sitting proud and happy in the front seat with Daddy through the double feature. Mama and Shacky, falling to sleep on top of each other in the back. The smooth, quiet drive home. Daddy and Mama going to bed together at the same time, happy just like on television. Mama coming in to listen to his prayers. Pushing sweet soft lips on his forehead after he had asked God's blessings for *everybody*.

"Good night. Sleep tight. Don't let the bedbugs bite." Mama leaving the door open just a crack. The boy waking up early for fried fish and grits before Sunday school. Daddy walking around in his underwear, laughing and funny.

"I don't call you son because you shine. I call you son because you mine."

Sitting on Daddy's lap while he drove the Lincoln down some back road. Hands on the wheel, feeling grown and little all at the same time. Neighbors asking for abc's and 123's. Daddy's pockets full of dimes and quarters for

"Now or Laters" and "Moon Pies." Uncle Enerst and Aunt Beck coming over for cards. Aunt Bessie, big-tittied and sweet-smelling, dishing out extra helpings of ice cream and lemon meringue pie.. Yes, that was it. All of it. The little brown family (little they say because Mama had stayed extra long in the hospital after the boy was born just to take care of that.). Daddy working, Mama working. The boy smart and funny, Shacky all Tomboy pretty. Strange, impossible that the boy has got it all mixed up now; that he can't figure out where all the good and the happy left off and the crying and the cussing, the disappointment and the evil began. Mama always said that things might have worked out if she could just have stayed at home. Just stay there and take care of Daddy, Shacky, and the boy. But Daddy never believed in none of that. Mama needed to work. Daddy's business was going good. He was cleaning more than twenty buildings, six days a week. Only Sundays and Saturday nights free. That's why he always went out like he did. A man needs time to himself after dumping garbage cans and scrubbing floors all week long. Mama never said exactly what she needed. Still, her job bought the furniture, and the trips to the beach, the school clothes, and the health insurance. That's why she had to keep working even when they switched her to nights and she had to leave every afternoon, Shacky and the boy half-crying while some teenaged neighbor-girl promised to warm up supper and make everybody wash their faces before bed.

People always said that Shacky took after her daddy, the boy after his mama. But of course there's no need to get into all that. What he can tell you for sure though is that his growing up wasn't as hard as you might think. It was just a little bit complicated.

For one thing they told him never to tell a lie, but *they* lied all the time. Matter of fact, they still do. And he doesn't mean lies about Santa Claus coming down the chimney when he knew that Mama had put all his toys on lay-a-way at the Kmart months before and then called herself hiding everything in the back of her and Daddy's closet a few days before Christmas came. Nothing as cute as that.

Instead they would go on about how he was supposed to grow up and be good and kind and God-fearing and innocent; how he was to do well in school and mind his manners so that everybody would smile nice broad smiles whenever they saw him at the grocery store or the barber shop. But he doubts that they ever really meant it. At least if they did they sure did seem to go out of their way to make certain that he had plenty to keep him from ever becoming what they said they wanted him to become.

Don't get me wrong. They loved the boy all right. Loved him sweet and hard all at the same time. It just looked like they couldn't exactly figure out what to do with him. They knew what to tell him, but like he said, they didn't seem really to believe the words that came out of their mouths. That might explain why the boy liked to talk so much, even when he communicated so little; why he kept to himself what he knew, letting people believe what they wanted about his always suspect abilities of comprehension.

It probably also explains why Daddy didn't bother too much with the boy besides occasionally pushing him on the swing or playing a few rounds of marbles, and of course the very occasional trips inside the Lincoln. The boy's daddy always knew that he wanted a son, one who might beg sips of beer, a bike, then later a car, a son who would play on the football team and chase girls till he finally got one pregnant and settled down to some regular life with a regular family. But *his* boy, no matter how much he tried to teach him boxing or take him with him to some backwoods bar to sit up on a stool and eat a pig's foot out of the big jar on the counter while he had a drink or two, didn't seem like he was headed for that type of life, a life for a son of his, a life that he might understand and put his arms around.

Sometimes he did try to talk to his son, to tell him that he'd never had a daddy himself; that the boy would have to grow up to be a man to take care of hisself plus a wife and children to boot. Even tried to break him from running around behind his sister. She was a girl. She'd have a husband and a house full of chaps before too long. But a boy, his boy, would have to make it on his own. Not to say that he wouldn't help him when the time came; get him set up in a house of his own, give him a couple of buildings to clean, introduce him around to his white folks.

Shiiit! Smart as he was that boy could really do something with the business; had the biggest cleaning service in Charlotte, if not all of North Carolina. But the boy was just still too little and tender hearted to understand everything that he'd like to explain to him. Would bust out crying if you hollered at him too bad, couldn't think about nothing but coloring books, and *The Wizard of Oz*, and *The Cat in the Hat*.

Looked like the best thing was to leave him alone then. His mama and sister would eventually wise him up. Nothing he could do with him now anyway. One thing was for damn sure though, the boy couldn't always stay fat and soft and cry-babyish like he was. Women might act stupid but they knew that boys have to grow up to be men. Of course he didn't want his son to be nasty or nothing, but he did want him to show folks that he had something of his daddy in him. Sometimes it seemed that one more stroke and he would have turned out to be a girl or at least funny. And he'd be Goddamned if he was going to put up with any of that. Not to worry though. Like he told his wife, the boy would soon enough be running down women. It was natural, had to happen. He was his son, wasn't he? He'd just have to figure all of that out on his own though, just like he had.

A man's got to learn all about abuse and shame, fighting and lying if he's gonna turn out correct. He knew the boy wasn't but a wee little thing, pushing his truck around, wearing his underwear out into the yard. Could be right odd when he wanted to be. Like that time, he got hold of that whole glass of rum and Coke his daddy had made for himself, thinking it was just a regular soda. Drank the whole thing down before anybody noticed. Slept from early that evening until damn well the next, his mama just fussing, his daddy and Shacky just laughing to beat the band.

Still it did seem that somebody really ought to talk to the boy, tell him what he needed to know. But his daddy with all his work and the mortgage and his trying to have some type of life himself never did seem to have enough time.

Same couldn't be said for the boy's mama though. She was one to stay on top of her children. She had prayed for a handsome son and a pretty daughter, one of each. She wanted her son to grow up to be somebody, maybe a doctor or a minister. But she was afraid that he had got off to a bad start. With the way she had gotten married and the way the boy's daddy was, she had to be careful with him. She knew something about how fragile life was. She knew enough to expect disaster, to look for it, to stand on the front porch with her eyes wide open, ready for what was certain to come.

So when the Coltrane sisters (Anita was the youngest) came over to the house to play in the yard and the older girl (Bonita they called her) decided that they should play house, no one would have much blamed the boy for doing what it was a boy's part to do. When Anita's older sister opened the door of the storage shed and told the boy to go inside with her younger sister, the same age but a shade or two darker than the boy, he of course obliged. Neither child really knew what to do though when the door closed on them, sealing them in with the lawn mower and the hedge clippers. They just stood there, dumb and close in the dark, no more scared or bored than was normal for plain brown children of seven or eight. Thus when Bonita jerked the door open in order to find the two caught up in some ugly, incriminating, act of childhood passion, what she encountered instead was two not particularly clever children, one brown and squat, the other pitch black and elegantly tall, grinning and blinking with dumb looks on their faces and cobwebs in their hair.

Still the boy understood somehow that something wrong, "grown" he might have said, had happened. He just didn't understand exactly what. But when his sister's friend, Necie, reported that she'd seen the boy and Anita go into the shed together he was clever enough to both panic and to keep his mouth shut. Shacky was clever too, threatening for months that she would tell Mama unless the boy became her slave. Thus a slave he became, running quick errands and handing over bits of money, those dimes and quarters that Daddy was always good for, sometimes making an irritated refusal, only to be brought back into line by his sister's threat that she would tell Mama about the shed, Anita, the Coletrane sisters, and the dark. That was of course until Mama overheard the girl's too loud, too cocky threats.

"Tell me what?!" Mama snapped one day, camouflaged behind some job of laundry or mopping that made her invisible to her ever battling children. Something ugly happened then. Nothing strange or particularly uncommon, but ugly all the same.

"Tell what?! I said." Mama's voice full of metal and salt alerting Shacky and the boy that soon enough all their secrets would be hers.

Of course Shacky broke first, relinquishing hold on the briefly established treasure of the boy's servitude, telling what she knew, or rather what she thought she knew. And Mama believed what she heard. She had expected that this day would come. She was prepared for it. All that fighting and cussing with Daddy had hardened her, made her ready for the betrayal of her sweet brown son, ready to dismiss the heavy crop of tears that gathered on his girlishly long lashes. She believed—she knew—that the boy was hiding something, something that had happened in the dark, something that she understood already, something that was elemental, intrinsic, part of the shock and pain of loving a boy. She insisted, moreover, that the boy admit his crimes, that he break himself into a thousand bitter little pieces that a woman might scoop up and keep hidden in a bin next to the trash. She wanted proof, proof from his own lips, that he too was just like his Daddy, just as mannish and nasty. She wanted the son whom she had long been promised, a boy who might burn in bitter sin before her, only to be turned, with force if need be, toward some cleansing light. So when he told the truth, the stupid, simple truth as he knew it: shed, darkness, long dull moments of close silence, sudden light, the banality and unknowing wonder of his play, Mama refused to believe him. Instead she got her belt and insisted that he tell again.

When he cried even louder she pulled her children into her bedroom, lay herself on her queen-sized mattress, belt in hand, Shacky looking on both triumphant and scared, as Mama threatened to whip the truth from the boy, into the boy, him sobbing out what seemed to her some ridiculous lie, acting much more stubborn and hard-headed than she had anticipated. Finally, she decided to trap the boy, sending her daughter to gather the evidence that would return clarity to her household. And behold, a bevy of preadolescent girls entered Mama's bedroom, all swearing to have seen the boy enter the shed with Anita, proof enough of some impossibly vulgar yet still unstated crime.

"Tell me what you did and you won't get a whoopin" Mama soothed.

183

"Nothin'" was not a proper answer. The boy stood his ground, hollering all the more when Mama flicked the belt against those ever thick thighs of his. He remained solidly defiant nonetheless, a beacon of lies in the midst of the burning, insinuating eyes of Mama, Shacky, and the encircling tribunal of the girls. Finally tiring of waiting for the boy to retreat from his own innocence, Mama came up with a clever idea. She instructed her daughter to go to her room to bring back a life sized pink/plastic doll that had long since been committed to some half attended corner. The naked form was laid on the floor, its synthetic blond hair billowing out behind its half shaved head, its legs impossibly askew. Mama told the boy to show her what he had done or face the lash. The boy refused. But another quick lick, this one heavy and to the point, changed all that. And so with enough sobbing and shame to turn the whole thing decidedly operatic the boy lay himself on the doll, rolling his hips in some impossibly ignorant rendition of "the nasty" about which he had heard so much whispered (especially from the ever so worldly Bonita Coletrane) knowing all the while that female eyes were looking on with strangely approving disapproval. He had it seems learned how to learn. Mama put away her belt then, the girls were dismissed, Shacky commended, but the story was trotted out for years whenever Mama wanted to embarrass the boy in front of school friends or stray relatives. His mama liked to keep pretty pictures of her children. This one would do fine.

W. K. Medlen

God's Blood

Shaking you held the tray of God's blood
but not out of fear
not content
exposing the seriousness in your brow
your eyes hung like bats

you cried during a Christmas church service
over a sermon you didn't particularly care for
you yelled "hoorah" when they recognized
the military
even though you were a mechanic for the air force

my grip on your truth is shaking

As a child I watched those
who had no fear of punishment
with envy
As a child I cried
out of embarrassment

I remember the smell of the
gloomy classroom staring
at the road darkened
by the clouds I anticipated
the end of the day doodled
played with my glue

my memories of childhood are shaky
like your hands on God's Blood.

The Story of Fathers

my dad was upset
stomping through his house
angry at the LEGOs in his way

his eyes were hanging like sleeping bats

my mother told me the story
one day around the kitchen island
grandma told her the story
about how my father's father
left marks

I screamed
I hate you
in the garage
the whole neighborhood
could hear

my voice tearing

they could hear
the generations of fathers
struggling
to tell the story
of their fathers
who beat them
who left marks
mountains

Cherri Randall

Daughter Rhymes with Laughter

Eye Rhyme

Palate is to plate as palace is to place. My ear rhymes daughter/water while my eye argues daughter/laughter.

Proper Nouns

The dictionary lists Cavalier as a noun before it's listed it as an adjective, but I sometimes wonder what Chevrolet was thinking when they named that car. I use cavalier as an adjective a lot more often than I use it as a noun. I know a lot more people with a cavalier attitude than I know cavaliers.

In a survey of British literature, I had to read the Cavalier poets, writers of witty and polished lyrics of courtship and gallantry. This was during the reign of Charles I, 1625 – 1649, during the English Civil War between the Cavaliers and the Roundheads. The Roundheads wore their hair short and did not support Parliament. I read the poems and passed the exams, but I never loved any literature that came between Shakespeare and Kate Chopin.

I would rather drive a Focus than a Cavalier, would take a Mustang over a Corvette. I like the idea of the word corvette—a highly maneuverable warship—but the naval theme can't compete with the Wild West linguistically. As if people buy cars based on words anyway.

I am driving a Focus because no one would finance me except the Ford Motor Credit Company when I was in grad school. The car is now paid off now, still running, and I doubt any other company will finance me. Although I am gainfully employed, my-free-credit-report.com shows student loans out the yin-yang.

The radio in the Focus is broken, some kind of metaphor for the lack of music in my life, but if it did work, the song that would come on at least once a day would be Kenny Rogers singing: *I told her someday if she was my girl, I could change the world with my little songs. I was wrong...* I don't want to write lyrics or change the world. But I wanted to entertain people and make them think with my words, and I wanted to drive a car that had a radio. That car is now only worth about $1,400.00 and I don't know if I could get financed again or not. I wanted my daughters to believe that I could write a book at least as good as the ones crowding the remainder tables after Christmas. My father, Lewis, was a Ford man.

My name is spelled wrong because my mother liked the name Sherry. Her name was Barbara Ann, just like the song, but she wanted me to be unique. I am frequently called Cherry or Cheryl and my maiden name was Owen without the "s." I was never happy about that until the band Alabama became famous and the lead singer's name was Randy Owen.

My mother wanted to name me Von Cherie. My father vetoed that name, and then she wanted to name me Cherie Lewis, like Shari Lewis, Lamb Chop's puppeteer, and thankfully he vetoed that. She named me Cherri Ann, after Barbara Ann, who had her first child in '62 and drove a '62 Chevy Bel Air, but not until 1965.

My father was a Ford man but I don't know why because the first truck I remember him driving was a late 50's model Chevy Apache. My mother had a '62 Chevy Bel Air, four-door, white sedan. This was about 1966. I was four, and my brother wasn't born for another two years. When my brother was born in 1968, we got our first Ford, a baby blue Galaxie. Evidently, someone at Ford liked alternative spellings as much as my mother.

Damon Lewis, a Greek name juxtaposed with his father's first name. I always felt he won the name lottery at our house. He had a cool name, correctly spelled, although when he was ten years old, the movie *Damien: Omen II* was released and even though we didn't have a movie theater in our town, he took a lot of flack over his name, Damon Owen, and almost everyone called him Damien with three syllables instead of two for years after that.

Periods

A period is a terminal mark of punctuation. A full pause made at the end of a complete sentence. A period is also a unit of time marked by the recurrence of some phenomenon or process. It's synonymous with age/era, as in the Elizabethan age, the Romantic era, or the Renaissance period.

Period is a versatile word, has definitions in music, geology, physics, astronomy, and mathematics. Like my brother's name, it is Greek, a compound of peri (around) and ode (suffix meaning way) and bears no relation to the Grecian Pindaric ode, a poem meant to be sung, *lyrics*. Period is not only a noun but can also be an adjective (especially drama: a period play, period costumes) and is also an interjection: a word used by a speaker or writer to indicate that a decision is irrevocable or that a point is no longer discussable.

It was my father's favorite interjection. NO DAUGHTER OF MINE IS GOING TO PARADE AROUND LIKE THE TOWN TRAMP, PERIOD. He interjected himself between me and the door. I thought of his edicts in

188

musical terms. If he was merely stating his laws, they were acapella, unaccompanied by the orchestra of his flailing arms and the ferocity of his flying spit. He was a smoker, and sometimes a drinker. We did not grow up with dental insurance, and the only visits to the dentist in my childhood were for extractions.

*

I got my first period when I was eleven years and seven months old and I wanted everybody to know except my father. I didn't know we were poor, that other kids got their teeth cleaned every six months and went out of town to the picture show sometimes. I wanted stick-on pads because that's what the other girls at school had and they made fun of my belts. When I begged for the stick-on kind, my mother told me to be thankful I had pads at all, to imagine what Indian women used one hundred years ago, to ponder what the women in the Bible did when they bled.

Sentences

The photograph of my parents' wedding is black and white. Nothing white except the cake and my mother's dress; nothing black except the suit my father is wearing. Now, after all these years the picture has faded to shades of gray. My mother posed in the foreground and my father stood behind her. They are not parents yet. She holds the knife poised above the cake with his hand clasped over hers.

By the time I turn twelve, the dress has yellowed to ivory and is stored in the huge basement closet of the house we live in. There is also a Valentine-pink ball gown, strapless, with rhinestone diamonds embedded across the bodice and layers of tulle over the satin skirt. A pair of acrylic high-heeled mules encrusted with diamonds accents the dress perfectly. Sometimes, when she is at work, I venture upstairs and get her dangly clip-on earrings that cascade diamonds down my neck. Even though they pinch my earlobes flat, I wear them so my ensemble is complete as I sing "Like a Rhinestone Cowgirl" for hours along with Glen Campbell's 45 rpm record on my orange plastic turntable. I was born for karaoke and *American Idol*, but I came thirty years too soon.

My mother stopped using her diaphragm a few months before I was conceived. My parents married on February 11, 1961, and I was born in June of 1962. My mother turned twenty the following September, and that January my father was thirty-four. During my entire childhood, she never breathed a single word of regret over my birth, but in my adulthood, we both said the words over and over.

If not for me, she could have left him. In fact, she did leave him, but she gave him the opportunity to follow, and he took it. She gave him that option as a father, not as a husband, but it was a package deal.

* * * * *

There is this one picture that I can never reconcile. She is standing next to her friend Patsy and they have taken a Greyhound bus from where they live in Las Cruces, New Mexico, headed for Odessa, Texas. My mother had turned eighteen, but Patsy had not. In this picture, my mother is six feet tall and blonde, whereas Patsy is a little brunette mouse.

Patsy's parents figure out that their daughter is running away and finds out from Greyhound where the bus will be stopping. The sheriff in Pecos gets called too late. My father is deputy sheriff in Monahans, Texas, and he asks Patsy's parents for a description since they requested that she be apprehended when the bus pulls in.

"She's with a tall blonde," her father tells my father. He is waiting for them when they step down from the bus.

My mother argues that she is eighteen and has her mother's permission to go to Odessa. He can arrest Patsy all he wants, but he has no business in her business.

"I need something to prove your age," he tells her. "Let me see your driver's license."

"I don't have one. If I did, I wouldn't be on the bus, now would I?" she sasses back.

"Wooooeee," he says. "I like a girl with a little bit of fire."

Patsy is shushing her, but my mother is not listening.

He laughs, puts them in cuffs and drives them to the station where they are booked.

*

They get their picture made in the cell and then my father takes them to get donuts and coffee, no cuffs. It is 300 miles to take them home, and it's a long dusty day to get there. They stop for gas and he gets them sodas. He doesn't complain when they want to go to the restroom in the next town. He takes his time getting them there and drops Patsy off first.

*

190

When they came back to Monahans because the guy in Odessa was a loser and because my mother was persuasive, Patsy has really turned eighteen and my father is almost finished with his divorce. As soon as it is legal, they are taking that picture with the wedding cake.

My father loved telling this story all his life. He rehearsed his timing until he could deliver a smooth narrative. When he told this story, he would leave out a lot of the details that I got only from my mother. There is not much Patsy in his version, more coffee, and his posturing about how he knew she was a spitfire from the moment the sun glinted on her blonde hair stepping out of that Greyhound.

I later asked my mother how she could look at a picture of herself in jail and then marry the man who arrested her. She looks at me, perplexed.

"That's not Patsy. That's Gracie."

"How did that happen?"

"That jail picture is not me and Patsy in Monahans. That's me and Gracie at the Otero County Fair. I'm only seventeen in that picture. The jail was a prop, and we got our picture made for a dollar."

I spent many years of my life thinking that picture was my mother in jail when it was really just my mother at the fair. It scares me that I may have made other assumptions about reality. My father would tell the story of how he met my mother to anyone who listened all their married life, and it always ended with the same punch line: "I put her in jail so she married me to get even. I've been serving my sentence ever since."

Dependent Clause

I have red hair, like Pebbles. My parents watched *The Flintstones* sponsored by Winston cigarettes which my father smoked because Winston cigarettes tasted good like a cigarette should. My mother smoked them too. I was eleven when she quit. The thing was, Wilma also had red hair, so Fred must have been carrying a recessive gene for Pebbles to show up with Irish or Scottish ancestry. I have red hair but my mother is blonde, my father more like Fred than I ever wanted to admit. I spent six years being daddy's girl and Momma was a footnote in the pages of my biography, all because he had to be Fred Flintstone.

People always assume I am Irish, and I like saying that I'm actually Scottish just to watch them fluster. My mother says I'm mostly Dutch on her parent's side and my father says his father was German and no one knows anything about his Heinz 57 mother. My grandparents were named Owen, Reed, Elmore and Baird.

When I was sixteen, my mother's sister, Francell, came to visit and my Uncle Kenneth let me drive his chocolate brown Mercedes 450 SL to the store. I waited patiently all day as my mother and aunt cooked, hoping they would discover any little pantry shortfall (vanilla, ketchup, Glad wrap), but there were no further opportunities to run an errand while the Mercedes blocked the rest of the cars in the driveway. I was just happy that Angie Schrick was working at the Quick Stop so it would be all over school Monday morning that she saw me drive to the Rock Station in a Mercedes. I was in love with Uncle Kenneth and my cousin Danny.

* * * * *

My mother married a deputy sheriff, but he had a family before ours. A former wife named Lucille and three children: Lonnie, nine, Nelda, seven, and Ginger, the baby was five. My mother would have the girls, Nelda and Ginger, while my dad was at work. Lucille would not send them any clean clothes to wear all weekend.

I want to write that my father was a good man for being the stable influence in his first three children's lives and my mother is a good woman for trying, at eighteen, to be a step-mother. My father had child support to pay to a first wife and had to take care of a second wife. Lucille didn't want a job and my father wished she would get one, whereas my mother was willing to work but he said no.

I want to say Uncle Kenneth was a good man for spending time talking to me, the hungriest child on the planet for words. I want to write that Lucille was a whore like my father said, and that I am a good girl who was as cute as a cartoon Pebbledy-Poo, also like my father said. But my non-fiction can only be so creative without crossing a million little lines and sometimes life goes beyond pebbles to pure rock hard and mostly poo. At forty-eight with two daughters in college, and sometimes when life is hard I tell them to sing the song that goes: *You don't always get what you want.*

My father was always something of a sportsman, so one night, chasing a few beers, he and another guy decided to go hunting out of season. They were busted jack-lighting deer, and that is what ended his career in law-enforcement.

They move to Odessa where they live in some rental property my grandfather Owen owns and my father works as a floor hand on an oil derrick. A fellow worker was in an accident on the job and got a huge settlement. Later, my father, unbeknownst to my mother, got the bright Flintstonian idea to stage an accident, but it went awry and he was really seriously injured. After that, my mother had to get a job and eventually my father had to be my babysitter. It wasn't destiny that made me daddy's girl, but proximity.

They ended up in the hospital at the same time, a heroic couplet. My father having back surgery and my mother having me, a chunky little redheaded dependent clause in a tragic play starring Dutch boys and Nazis.

Judith Serin

Some Family Stories

Grandmother and Grandfather Goldis in Odessa

Your cousin sends you a photograph she has restored and copied for your mother's relatives: Grandmother and Grandfather Goldis in Odessa. It is a studio photograph, taken around 1900, with the standard props—an ornate chair, a basket of flowers, a misty gray background that must be painted on a screen—and the dark clothes of the period with high collars, long sleeves, his wide lapels and elaborate tie, her cinched waist and many small buttons catching the light.

But look at their faces. These are not antique shop Edwardian ancestors. She is more striking with flat wide cheeks and the Asian eyes that made your mother say when she went to Japan that everyone looked like her relatives. Her lips are full in a way that is fashionable now but wasn't when you were a child and had full lips too. Her gaze is open and strong, extraordinarily present, and her hair pulled back from her narrow forehead is thick, unruly.

At first your grandfather looks more ordinary, but then you notice the long high-bridged nose, the strong mouth, the emphatic eyebrows. And their hands. His are broad, large for his body, peasant hands that he places confidently on his thigh and stomach. Hers are softer, narrower. One gently grasps his shoulder; the other curls nonchalantly around the basket of flowers. What happened to her? How could such a definite young woman become the bitter recluse in the family stories?

Looking at them now, you are proud of them and you decide to heal an old hurt. When you were in college, a Ukrainian girl told you that your mother's family weren't Ukrainian; they were Jewish. She said it with a tinge of derision that she probably didn't notice. Now you know another Ukrainian girl, a beautiful redhead with huge hazel green eyes who shows you a book of pictures of Odessa. You bring her the photograph. As you tell her the story from college, you see a silver star of David at her neck.

Your Sister Buys a Bra

She has always looked older than you. This is a source of distress until your twenties. At eleven she has the prominent bust of your grandmother, and your mother takes her downtown to buy a bra. You, at thirteen, don't need one.

At dinner your mother suggests that your sister show her bra, and she prances out in it. You don't realize how much this bothers you at the time; but later, when you are twenty and bra-less and the family is on vacation together, you pull off your dress in front of them all to change. Your parents are uncomfortable and tell you. You are embarrassed, then angry, remembering the scene at the dinner table when they admired your sister, and knowing you were only asking for your turn.

Your Father Frightens Your Sister's Boyfriends

After dinner he sits on a couch and thinks about his work. The family is used to his abstraction. Your sister is popular in high school, has boyfriends who come to pick her up in the evening. They are star athletes, class presidents, but they stand awkwardly inside the door, ready to bolt. You notice their lankiness, their pimples. When they see your father on the couch scowling, they are afraid of him. They don't know that he hardly noticed them.

The evening of your sister's prom, though, your father gets out the camera. One of the boys he'd frowned at arrives carrying a corsage. You run out to watch the couple posing for their picture on the lawn, you sister with the flower pinned on a long white dress with a pink velvet sash. You will insist on a long dress for your wedding.

Photograph of Walter Griffin at the Pool

You get out a magnifying glass to study his face under the pool-side table's umbrella. Yes, he is amazingly handsome; you weren't wrong, though now he is shorn of his power to wither your heart. But there he is—one boy—blond, tan, muscled, a champion swimmer—sitting at the table with five girls. He's fifteen or sixteen, the girls that age or younger. Your sister sits next to him, wearing sunglasses but you recognize her bathing suit. That and something familiar in her chin-line, her pose, the placement of her arms and hands as she writes. She's the only girl who isn't looking at him. Walter glances down, perhaps at what she's writing. He's smiling, clasping his hands, sheened with all that feminine attention, protected by the shield of his handsomeness from your lust and longing. Is that your back in the dark one-piece bathing suit? Maybe you're not there.

Snakes

Sometimes your family's cats trap garter snakes, but can't catch them; they're afraid of the head with its flicking black tongue, so they attack the tail. When the snake whirls to strike, the cat circles to the tail again—a fast, jerky *pas de deux.*

When you find them, you know to pick up the snake right behind its head, so it can't strike. You bring it in and put it in an old glass terrarium your mother covers with a piece screen held down by books at the corners. You'll let it out after a few days. But one snake pushes a book off and escapes, vanishing.

All winter a neighbor refuses to enter your house. Then one day in spring, its hibernation over, the snake slides out of the coat closet. Your mother opens the front door and it slips into its world.

Barbara Lewis

Time Exposure

I call this picture "The Happy Family." Ignore the shrieking baby, the snarling boy, the bellowing lady. There on the deck that luminous afternoon, life was pretty sweet. Everything I'd longed for was mine—a warm-blooded husband who didn't mind when I farted, funny babies, our very own house tucked into the hill, even fat hair and a tan. All that other stuff lay ahead.

Bob had not yet fallen out of love; Josh, my stepson, hadn't yet branded me as evil; and that afternoon, at least, my breasts were still attached to me, full to bursting, not yet floating in a jar somewhere on a laboratory shelf. On that shimmering August day, I was still on top of the world.

Bob would emerge from his fugitive amnesia, Josh and I would reconcile, and Dr. Kay Young worked artistry with an implant, but that shining piece of time had passed. No more fat hair, no more golden tan. My crinkly skin has paid the price. Our children now have children of their own.

The other day Josh's four-year-old daughter observed, "Grandma, I have light-brown hair, and you have light-white hair." I'll take it. Charlotte is a stickler for specificity, and light-white sounds a lot prettier than gray. Meanwhile our daughter reports that five-year-old Nico asked recently who loved him more, "God or Grandma." I'm in pretty good company. Doesn't God have light-white hair too?

Shelly Clark Geiser

Writing the Memoir

Start naming names,
promote a walking tour
through a town full of ghosts.

Load up bedraggled, exhausted families:
mothers, brothers, aunts and uncles,
drive them to the country,

dump them onto a dusty road
under the noon-white sun.
Pull their pants down around their ankles.

Keep stripping layers: bat, belt, finger, zipper,
this is where the old sick father comes in
and the alcoholic brother, his trembling hands.

Next, a complete chapter for the mental-breakdown mother,
tweezing every hair from her head until it resembles
the naked light bulb above the bathroom sink.

Shave off the ugly hairy belly
of your boyfriend who is in love with himself.
Do it while he is sleeping.

Expose the kooky astrologer,
her psychic hot line single-handedly
keeping the lonely alive.

Dig deeper now,
there's probably an abortion somewhere
and institutional therapy.

Finally, in the climatic last chapter
take care of what's left:
tattoos, scars, the self-inflicted burns.

Now, the audience is in a frenzy, cheering in pain—
go ahead, eat all the way to naked bone,
slash every reachable vein.

Rebecca T. Dickinson

We Never Said Hello

She died too soon. It's a selfish thing to think, especially since I didn't know her. Very selfish. I still think she died too soon. Possibly too young. She was seventy-nine-years-old. Up until the last two months of her life, she pressed and kneaded dough, wiped flour on her apron, and made lunch for her husband every day when he arrived home from his store.

Ben drove to his parents' house and visited with her. I imagined them sitting at the table: Ben sipped on his coffee, and his mother served him some of her biscuits. *Those biscuits.* Ben loved her biscuits.

Mine will never be like hers.

If I've learned one thing from all of my relationships, no matter how great my recipe is it can't be as wonderful as my boyfriend's mother's meal. I make my lasagna with ricotta cheese. Ben and my father prefer it with cottage cheese, because that is how their mothers had made it.

No one is at fault for her death, except for maybe Ben and me. It's certainly not *his* fault.

Maybe if I had let him die her heart would've let her live. Maybe if I'd gone to my scheduled appointment in Winston-Salem...no, my soul would've died.

Last spring, Ben left his wife and told the rest of his family about his affair with a younger woman and his baby boy. Since then, his other four children slam all respect for him in the dumpster. His family closes the vault on him, the baby and me.

"My sister told me, 'You had nine months to tell us and you didn't. We have nine months to get through all of this.'"

What man wants to deal with two angry families and an emotional, pregnant woman all at once?

I remember Ben and I had already settled drama with my family by the time he had to tell his parents, brother, sister and children. One day his mother was in full health, and a few months later she died. Ben's brother and sister requested I not come to the December funeral.

Now the baby crawls, stands, claps and giggles while she rests in her grave. Today, the soft dirt covering her body will hold him up. It's the only time she'll carry the weight of the grandson she'd never meet.

I pull into a downtown parking spot. The main street is split in the middle by train tracks. Although the railroad station is long gone, small town commerce of the mid-twentieth century etches itself in the bricks of flat top buildings. One of the last stores to carry local-made clothes hides in between two cityscape trees. For decades, millworkers had spun yarn and made clothes for the town, but with the decay of the economy and business moving factories to China and Mexico the small two-window shop is all that remains.

I remember the coffee shop as my favorite place to sit, drink a mocha *crappichino*—as Ben calls it—perform my interviews, or write one of my stories for the town's newspaper.

These days, I'm a homemaker and writer pulling my son's stroller out of the back of my green Ford Escape. It still shows the stickers of my college-girl past. A faded pink Palmetto tree and quarter moon peel off in the corner and my University of South Carolina parking sticker is plastered on my back window.

The stroller weighs the amount of two, four-month-old twins.

I wait for the traffic lights to turn red, and I push my baby across the street to the flower shop. Pink and white dogwoods bloom all around us, and a man cleaning windows tells me he hopes winter doesn't return. The ground hog had been wrong, he says. After all, spring arrives in late February on the border of the Carolinas.

I still feel like a newbie American spy in Russia. The bureaucratic government – just a fraternity of former KGB members – sends someone to watch me. But there isn't anyone with big, black binoculars hiding on top of buildings. *Come on,* I say to myself, *not many people in this town remember me.* I had only worked for its hometown newspaper for a short time.

Most likely no one recalls my name. Still, my heart beats faster, nerves crawl up and down my spine like spiders, and I'm aware many natives know Ben and his family. His father had opened his own store in the late 1960's, and now his younger brother runs it.

Outside the flower shop, a woman, with a crop of white hair, talks in her mechanical voice and yellow throat tube to a larger lady. I notice from my former work experience as a small town journalist many rural areas had lost their businesses. But here, people walk up and down the street on a sunny day, and there is talk of more restaurants to come and fill up vacant buildings.

I feel as if I entered a rich grandmother's parlor. Flowers in beautiful white vases decorate every corner. They're everywhere, like waiters at a restaurant ready to serve you. Plants make me nervous. They always die in my care. I usually forget when to water them.

In the first grade, I remember everyone's plants grew faster than mine. My brown stem remained a short, brown stem.

"How may I help you ma'am?" the lady at the counter asks.

"Yes ma'am, I ordered some roses yesterday."

"Of course, I have them right here. Would you like a card?"

"Yes ma'am, please," I reply.

She places two bright red roses wrapped in green paper and a red ribbon on the counter. I wish I had ordered something larger, but I don't even know the difference between flowers one buys for a wedding or a funeral.

"Sometimes simplicity is better," Ben had said to me.

I also wonder how I'll keep the roses on the grave. While it has warmed up, wind kicks up a notch blowing my hair in every direction when I'm outside.

Ben will meet me in a little while, and he'll know how to keep them in place.

The lady hands me the card.

I write … *What do I write? What can I write?*

Ben's sister visits their mother's grave once a week. She'll see them, and I wouldn't want to upset her. She's already upset enough with her brother because her second husband had left her for a younger woman.

> *Dear Grandma,*
> *I love you very much, and I know you will watch over me*
> *from heaven.*
> *Love,*
> *James*

After the lady pins the card to the ribbon, I place them on James' stroller. Cars rev up and run down the street. I guess school had let out early. A few teenagers race a jeep through all three lights.

It reminds me of Ben's two older sons: one away at college, and the other embracing everything high school offers. Freedom. Freedom from boring adults and a father, who as Ben says, they believe is the devil.

"Neither one will pick up the phone or return my texts," Ben says.

My heart swells. I want to cry. As with his mother, I know there isn't anything I can do. The only thing I could've done to save the boys and Ben's mother from the truth is to have gone to Winston-Salem.

Ben would still have his other two boys. They would remember their father loves them, and everything he's done for them.

I hurry across the street. The wind blows the roses off the stroller and they fall on the ground. I pick them up and make sure every petal is in its place. Petals are so delicate, like butterfly wings. It's a fearful beauty. Once one touches it, and a petal, a wing breaks apart. I don't want to divide any sector from its creation.

James laughs and giggles as he swats his green frog rattle hanging on his car seat.

"Eeee-he-he agagaga," he says.

I am so thankful that I hadn't gone to Winston-Salem in October 2009.

My father always says an abortion is between the girl, her doctor and God. I believe every woman deserves the right to make her own choice.

While I drive to the cemetery, I remember thinking it was my only option.

I recall a journalist picking up one more wine bottle with each car accident, deadly or not. I'd grown sick of myself covering the injured and dead. *Sick* of right wing nut jobs, who blame people like me for America's problems. *Tired* of pretending to love a jealous and angry husband, who always cornered me. I think sometimes I should've done something else. But, I'd already spent years writing everyone else's story. The time had come for me to walk in the footprints of my own.

"You're going to get rid of it right?" my ex-husband said to me. "Right?"

I left my sexless marriage, and the job I once longed for. My college friends dropped me like a penny in the sewer, and hell opened its jaws.

"When we do this," Ben had said me, "it'll be us against the world like two men in a bar fight. I'll have your back and you'll have mine."

I park my car on a hill. Ben pulls in behind me and carries James to his mother's head stone. An early spring breeze picks up throughout the cemetery.

"They didn't put those roses in a vase of some kind?" he asks.

"They wrapped in green paper. I guess I should've asked for one."

"It's okay. If you hold him, I'll find something."

When Ben returns from his car, he bends part of a clothes hanger and forks the roses at the foot of her grave.

I sit with James beside her flat grave marker. I pull out my cell phone and take a picture of James playing next to his grandmother's headstone. The phone camera captures the late afternoon sun as it gleams over the baby boy and his grandmother.

James puts grass in his mouth and I catch it. He giggles and taps the ground like it's a judge's desk.

"He's got her red hair," Ben says.

I never thought I'd give birth to a red-head child. Maybe that's God's sweet vengeance on me.

"Well, James, this is your grandmother," I say, *whom you could've met had her heart held up.* "I bet she loves you very much."

That's a strong gamble. I don't have anything to bet with except Ben's promise she does love James.

I didn't mean to cause you this pain, I say to her. *I know it wasn't right the way things happened, but I love your son very much. Ben's a great man and father and James is a good baby.*

"Soon," Ben says. "The rest of them will come around soon."

His mother was coming around *soon* to the idea to meet her youngest grandson last fall.

Soon crashes like a star from heaven into the ground.

"Yeah ... I hope so."

James gurgles and picks more grass on her grave.

Monica Macansantos

James

Dots of light flicker between the leaves and tendrils of your foster mother's backyard garden. Two figures emerge from the dusk of memory. You are the white skinned, dark-eyed, restless teenager, chasing the smaller, dark-haired, brown-skinned child.

The dining room lamp is switched on. Dinner is about to be served, and your foster mother and my parents are waiting. But we don't return indoors, not yet. We prefer to stay outside, chasing each other until the darkness snatches our figures away from each other's sight.

Despite your rough-and-tumble way of playing tag, you never chase me into your foster mother's unruly garden. "There are snakes in there," you tell me, repeating, perhaps, what your foster mother told you (minus the heavy French accent). I don't need to be warned. My fear of the dark is enough to keep me away.

When night falls, we return to your house, where your foster mother gives you a stern look before telling you to set the table. She complains about your slowness. Your name rings in the air as brightly as the lamp that hangs, like a golden, basketed fruit, over the table.

"Ja-mes, your hands are dirty."

"Ja-mes, go get the ice cream."

You narrow your eyes and fall silent.

You retreat to your room after dinner. She speaks to my parents of the liquor that fed you in the womb, of your slowness at school, of your rock-hard stubbornness that can only be cracked open by your rage.

You laugh your heart out the next time we visit you. Your fingers dance under my armpits and your name rings in my throat when I scream in protest.

On our next visit, you are gone from that house of musty, doily-covered furniture, of vines that are never trimmed. We listen to your voice as it bodies forth from a telephone receiver, from a state school in the big city.

Your foster mother winces as she holds the phone to her ear, and I can see how your words sting. But your voice turns gentle when the receiver is handed to me. Your words float from the static and I cling to them, wondering whether even your breath will be muted, snatched away.

My family has since returned to our country. Years after my parents receive your foster mother's final letter to them, I imagine you a grown man, walking

208

down a darkening city street, your eyes turned down, never speaking, never making these scenes in my mind seem real.

What seems more real is your impish grin and your dark eyes laughing, brightening the room of memory, the same way in which, perhaps, that dinner lamp, if someone still switches it on, brightens that lonely, dusty house, faintly illuminating that dark, unkempt garden, reaching into the hollows of those bushes, until the eyes of snakes, touched by the light, begin to shine.

Richard Ballon

That Green Land of Light and Shadow

Billy, that green summer when the twilight swept the herd of deer onto the lawn, the roses had climbed the trees to watch, and hung like red beads in the larch. The glade below murmured with bees rolling in the foxglove as you and I sat, plunked in each eye of a broken window, our feet knock knocking the side of the house. Your hand reached across that space and the first time we held hands was three stories high, ah that we could have jumped and landed in a different world where goodbye would be a word unknown.

Paul Sohar

The River

A klutz, a nerd, a nobody; all these words have been applied to me from early age. A child prodigy of failure. Our electronic age confirms this public perception, awarding me a PhD in incompetence. It all started when I flunked out of nursery school; I just stood by the door crying until mom picked me up. All through first grade I struggled unsuccessfully to write a cursive "a" and to tie a bow. I was clearly unfit for this life. But how could I avoid it? Run away from home? War intervened, and we all had to run away from the bombardment to a small town, not worth holding. The defending army quietly withdrew with the authorities and social services such as feeding refugees. Mom suffered the hardest, refusing to share her salami with me, saying children could endure starvation better than grownups. The conquering army added to the anarchy but not to the food supply. Our overcrowded building had a large general store in front, shuttered, apparently abandoned; I smashed the back door with an ax, followed by a mob. I devoured the scoop of flour I found in a drawer and one stray egg. My followers found nothing. With the ax still in hand I smashed the cash register and, staring down my fellow robbers, I pocketed the rich hoard. My passport to freedom was useless in the chaos though, and after a few months my mother wheedled it out of me, saying we needed to buy food. My lifesaver gone, I had no way out except suicide. I did it a few years later by jumping into a deep river. In imagination, I gave up life, became like a twig adrift, but I kept my consciousness to see where the river was going. Still looking.

Gina Ferrara

Money, Mississippi (1966)

The tarnished scent, a silent trumpet
of fumes entered windows
when the engine stopped.
I shared the backseat with my sister
in the gold Oldsmobile
that passed the delta like a humming comet.
The car sputtered, after several attempts
and rhetorical turns,
the white needle affixed to empty,
a stuck pendulum, on a dirt road of namelessness.
My father tucked three dollars
inside his black sock to walk
to Money, Mississippi...my mother
spotted him first—
silver haired, carrying a copper can
flaked in rust. The stranger arrived
without any obvious albatrosses.
Coveralls, faded, nearly cerulean,
supported by matchbook-sized brass buckles—
pointing his astute finger toward the opaque, empty fields
as love bugs stuck to the windshield
with a small specificity.
Black boys get lynched he rasped,
a pack of Pall Malls tucked inside
a slack pocket.
My father began removing his shoe
to give him money.
The stranger placed his hand
on my father's shoulder
where it rested larger than a lily.
He gazed at our faces, pale, upturned,
the rhythm of sleep—
dreamful and dreamless,
not stirring as the cicadas
grew louder, more fervent with their vespers.

Keep driving he urged. Money,
Mississippi pressing against my father's heel
as he turned the ignition.

Martha Everhart Braniff

Humming Birds at Midnight

At night I listen to the branches of a bottle brush graze and scratch, clawing on the screen of my open window. The shrub billows forth red feathered blooms attracting humming birds.

I am a child, and I love the birds. Sometimes I am a bird-child.

Maybe, if it isn't the bottle brush scratching in the fury of night, it could be, yes, it could be whiskers against my cheek, and Father's fingers, the shape of white cigars, cracked and coarse, his breath laced with nicotine, and Mother watching, a distant gloom who hides in icy corners.

My cry dissolves through the screen of my window, where whir of wings and shadows play outside my room, but there is no deliverance for me. My spirit flees into the bottle brush where lesser children live among the humming birds. Lesser children, stooped and spent, but still alive.

* * * * *

Run, Brother, run. They're after you, today. Surely someone in suburbia will save us if we make it to the yard. And if we do, we must be careful of the thorns that fall from a huisache tree. Thorns, sharp enough to prick the belly of a dying humming bird.

* * * * *

In Catholic school, there is hope if I kneel on my rosary, kneel for lacerating hours to endure a penance for the sins of—

Father, Mother, you can stop if you go and get some friends. Stop! Stop playing crooked- puzzle games amid the smoke of cigarettes.

Hum, hum, a chorus in my head frets and frets. Listen. You can hear it, too, humming birds among the thorns.

* * * * *

When the doors are locked, we children hide from those who prick us, bleeding from the bottom of our souls.

But in the end they find us in the dark, and the only thing that offers peaceful parcel or a pittance of reprieve are the humming birds at midnight, holy noise in my ear.

Gregg Weatherby

Approaching Home

From a block away
even before the traffic signals
on the corner by the station
the bus horn
sets those departing
running.

The clerk
who seems to dream
and live
by his cigarettes and coffee
tells which passengers
must depart now
or wait.

This is your greeting then
to the wet town. If
you care enough
to sit, you will find
the molded plastic cold or
you may wait outside
for your guts to stop
moving
the way they have learned
from buses
only to find
even on the slatted benches
the rain
has found places to collect
your cardboard suitcase
turned to washboard sides—

It will warp, that is
before you know it
your clothes will be wet
falling out into streets or
country highways.

Mom's Chair

I wish she could have gone on
those last days at home
rocking easy
her favorite chair
old glide rocker

rescued from the damp garage
cobwebs leaves mildew
now
my reading chair
comfortable
as talking to mom
rock easy

see her here
doing the Sunday Times crossword
knitting reading
short-term memory
gone to pieces
her drugstore glasses
never quite right
cushions soft
on her old back
rock easy

I wish she could have gone on
rocking easy
now I sit here
see her sometimes
rock easy

Old House Winter

When we moved in
the house was huge
compared to the old farmhouse
and the small frame in town

magically too
it grew the sunporch
became dining room
a table of preposterous proportions
a new deck was added
herb pots and geraniums
mom's flowers
keeping watch
even the trees
stood taller

I couldn't wait to get out
but it was not
what I thought

after me
the rest followed
one after another
(I don't remember the order)
until all five were gone then
the house shrunk in on itself

the dining room table
became covered with newspapers
toys and games in case
the grand kids came over
(dad often bewilderingly
ate his meals at the counter)
the mail piled up
with weeks of crosswords

this time of year
dad sealed the cracks
around doors and windows

and complained of the cold
mom cooked large meals
he didn't like leftovers

as the rooms were closed off
it became harder to get out
the doors seemed to lead nowhere
and all their friends
turned to ghosts

they took their turns
in hospital beds in i.c.u.s
hospice care for mom
until they couldn't go back
and left far from their bed

snow deep on the walk
herb pots lie broken
on the back porch
my brother turns the lights on
against burglars
but each night
the old house goes dark

Equinox

First day of spring
means nothing here
the earth starts its tilt
towards the sun
lake effect
flakes fly from the northwest
the late night silence of snow offers
three to five inches
of no accumulation
the sky gray
for days

and the light
   (what there is of it)
throws its blanket
over potential brilliance
of snow
fog is the angels' share
and the willow dips its fingers
into the stream

no
significant sun
for days now the
windows rattle in their frames
whether we like it or not
the earth bows to spring
in its own good time

Ashes

The tulips bloom untended
a year after she passed
why am I amazed
what moves but me
through the old house
handling blankets towels
helpless with old photos
what to do with sketchbooks
paints easel her old robe
folded neatly in a box

why do I wonder
what was saved this ceramic this
picture the dried flowers in a book

why handle all these old
boxes these
legacies of dust

Sweet Water

When the days warm and the nights still cold
we'd go to the sugar bush
in the hollow down the hill
and run the metal buckets back
through the snow and mud
dump them in the seemingly towering tank
on top of the heavy wooden sled
pulled by a pair of old draft horses
icy water filling our boots sodden
mittens sagging
we didn't mind
we'd warm up in the sap house
smells of sweet steam and wood fire
boiling hot dogs
in one of the rows of evaporating pans
eating the thick syrup on the snow
a lifetime ago it seems
when there was white smoke
in the dark gray woods each spring
and the mark of heavy horseshoes
in the undisturbed snow
the unused dirt road

Noelle Sickels

The Hedge

We called it, simply, the hedge. Neglected, tough, ever green, it stood thick and glossy-leaved along the side of the house next to the neighbors who, in fair weather, kept their cheerful, golden toddler all day in a playpen in the driveway, a child whose beauty so far excelled the mien of his homely siblings and downtrodden parents that my mother insisted he must have been brought by fairies or, at least, been the outcome of one unexpected night of transcendent passion. My mother believed in such things. Fairies. Passion. Their fruited gifts. Their taxes.

The hedge and the wall of our house formed a narrow corridor from the mailbox to the kitchen steps and door, and on past the door to the clothesline under the trees—a chute from the street and my mother's small rock garden out front to the back yard, from which you could descend into the cool, shadowy cellar, a realm of sawdust and my father's perfect tools and, on Sundays, opera from the radio.

In season, the hedge's generous sprays of white blossoms emitted a delicate perfume detectable yards away, an unreasonable scent that evoked a strange blend of melancholy and elation close to homesickness, though I had not yet begun to imagine any other place or time. When the hedge was in bloom, I would enter the house only by the kitchen door, reaping the smell, intoxicated with mysterious yearning.

Yesterday, on a sidewalk fifty years and 3000 miles away, I was startled by the sudden and insistent proximity of that familiar scent. I couldn't locate the source, but I was transfixed, unwilling to move out of its range. The yearning that hadn't fit in the long-ago burgeoned into aching, proper life. Again I sit shucking corn on the wooden steps outside our kitchen. It's summer, of course—in memory, childhood seems always to happen in summer or in the snow. Again I hear the soft babble of the fairy boy next door and the louder hum of bees among the hedge flowers. The old street is at my back, ahead a corner of clothesline in view, white diapers flapping. Strains of "Carmen" ride the humid air like spiderlings. The steps are warm and splintery beneath my bare feet. Corn silks litter my Bermuda shorts.

I am happy but I want to cry. It is all too sweet, too gone, too deceptively simple, like the reach of the hedge's cloying scent beyond its rooted stems, beyond its sturdy, screening leaves.

Alba Poku

Father's Affair

His mouth, a stale cracker, dry, cracked.
I can't believe that five dollars and a small white rock
could cause such an addiction.
Fire red veins in his eyes, gazed at me with the pattern of a jigsaw puzzle.
White milky residue substance aligns his eyes
thick and gooey like vanilla cake frosting.

Avoiding eye contact with me—a teenage boy being caught sneaking back in the house at 3:00 in the morning. His ashy frail hands began to tremble. He could have been a guitarist playing an imaginary guitar.

He shuffled past me unsteady with an awkward rock back and forth. His clothes smelled of rotten cheese and bile mixed together. He reached into the old maple wood cupboard and pulled out his repenting tools: an old black leather Holy Bible, a sinful red Bic ink pen, and a fresh white sheet of notebook paper.

As he positioned himself carefully at the child-sized wooden desk, an image of death flew past me. I never really wanted to acknowledge this deep dark secret. Every time I think about the preacher exiting his body and the demon entering...my stomach turns. This is a never-ending nightmare that sporadically invites itself into our home.

The room grew quiet after a few seconds later and all I could hear was his pen scribbling on the thin white paper. The sound of the pen writing against the notepad reminded me of how hard his lifestyle must be. I stood erect in front of him like a statue, and I stared at him with a look of pity. He refused to make eye contact with me. Instead, he bit his bottom lip as hard as he could while transparent tears flowed down his cheeks. No words were exchanged between us, just the sound of the scribbling against the notebook paper in preparation for his Sunday morning sermon.

Margaret Elysia Garcia

Shalom Ma Ze

(the lucid dream)

It used to happen frequently. Especially when I'd try to spend as many hours sleeping as I could—which was never really more than four. I slept on my side, exhausted, drooling. Drop dead tired. I imagine looking like the murder victim—exhausted angles of flesh and hair finally at rest, laid out awkwardly. When I realized the pattern, the circumstances I'd have to be in to get to this place, I got scared. I tried to quit getting too exhausted to sleep or too drunk to sleep, or too drugged to sleep because it's disturbing as hell to lay there—suddenly awake and watching as part of you drifts off and flies away while your body can't move. Part of me would lie there eyes open staring at my hands and trying in vain to will them to lift up and touch my face, but they just stay there dead. Unmoving.

In my dreams the same thing happens every time. A wave of something washes over me. My skin tingles, alert and scared. A deep low voice threatens me with death or dismemberment. Or more accurately threatens me with separation. My body will stay here dead among the pillows and comforter. My spirit will make the journey. My soul begins to fight with devils and angels on the way to hell. No one has told me anything, but when this starts to happen something in me goes towards preservation. The low voice cannot be good. He whispers in my ear but it reverberates in my chest and the pit of my stomach. He gets louder and louder and my voice goes softer and softer and I know somehow that if I quit quietly screaming, if for a moment my voice isn't there at all and his remains, then I'll have lost myself for ever—or at least the parts of me that are floating out there.

He tells me to join us. Join us, he says, and with the low baritone comes a shadow of swirling black wing beckoning. The Underworld awaits. It's quiet there, I can tell. People get to sleep. Women are no longer ripped into three pieces at night and a thousand in the day. It is a restful place, this place without my voice.

I can feel my spirit traveling. I'm allowed to see. She flies just over the treetops, just over the crest of the waves, just over the freeway overpass. She travels to places I cannot go anymore. She takes a running jump from my body. Floats and flies. Tonight she visits my grandmother. She sits across the street on the rooftop of the school across the way and watches. Yesterday she went to the desert looking for a man she barely knows. She flies over the grey

224

Atlantic to Germany she sits on the orange rooftops and watches the cobblestone ice up for the night. She goes there a lot. She hears late night bar brawls in gasthauses and early morning saws at the town butchers. She hangs in the cemeteries.

I pull back into my body when I think the spirit has stayed too long away and won't find her way back. I become a Catholic again for a moment. My mouth can't move but I'm reciting the Hail Mary. If I can make it through the prayer, I tell myself, I'll live. My spirit will come back and my soul will stop its way down to Hell. My face will stop twitching and my limbs will move. I'm only Catholic in my dreams now. I panic when I forget the words. I start over and over again with the Hail Mary. I get to the end and I get it right this time. "Blessed is the fruit of thy womb, Jesus." There I said it. I didn't say it out loud but it was a complete uninterrupted thought in my thought-filled head. They might let me out now. God is on my side; I just proved it. The deep voice is angry and my body rocks—I want to go back I think to it. Back. Bring me back. I'll bring myself back. I tell it. I know where all the parts of me are. We are coming together, this puzzled body. I can move a finger. A toe. My open eyes can close.

I enter my body again. Everything is there. Everything tired from the journey. I get up and look out the window and drink the water from the glass on the floor by the bed. I don't want to remember, but I keep trying harder to do so anyhow.

I work backward. I was going to the Werms cemetery in that particular dream. The stepfather used to like to take me there.

The stepfather and I had an ongoing outing, we had no traditions but since this occurred more than a few times, I have no choice but to call it ours. He liked to take me to cemeteries in Germany. The cemeteries of Germany seemed odd to me. I was used to big sprawling southern California ones that share the manicured hillside with coyotes, tarantulas, and those big giant metal oil-seeking crickets pumping up whatever dinosaur juice is left to the surface. My mother and grandmother used to take me there for picnics. I'd walk up and down the Queen of Heaven Cemetery while they talked. I'd do the math for every grave and see how long everyone lived. Babies and homeboys are buried in the short spaces by the curbs. I'd jot down odd names to use for stories. I'd read the gravestones. Everyone is belovedly generic in death: Father, Brother, Son, Solider. Everyone is hanging with Jesus. Is there nothing else to do? Is there nothing else to be?

There are the graves that have all information entered for the woman but the death date. The husband is there waiting for her. It's his plot. Literally, figuratively. She just needs a date and it is done. When I'm with my grandmother and my mother, they clean Dean's grave. They don't talk about him, they just clean and pull weeds and have me fetch fresh water and watch out for frogs jumping out from the plastic holders waiting for flowers. I look around at other graves. I wonder when his grave will be like the others around here, unattended and overgrown. The earth taking him once again farther back and away from them; the spirit and body separated for good.

The German graves in contrast are always meticulous. A family doesn't buy a plot for eternity, they just lease it for awhile. It's up to families to keep them up and keep them looking beautiful and meticulous and shiny. If the family cannot afford it anymore a new owner is interred on top with new engravings and new markings. The one who couldn't keep up payments is buried for good underneath with no marking or name to call attention to his or her bones and ash. The flowers are always fresh and no one is ever actually in a German cemetery. I imagine in the dead of night, Omas and Opas from every village awake and clean the walls and stones and set fresh flowers before anyone wakes. There were two cemeteries in our village and both were like this: meticulous death in black formal stones with bright fresh flowers.

But that's not where the stepfather liked to take me. He took me to the Jewish cemetery. When he first suggested it, I thought he was making a cruel joke or threatening, as he'd done before, to drop me off at Dachau where he said I belonged. Or worse, he'd send me on a train to Poland. I didn't know what that meant when I was eleven, twelve, but since then I've ridden trains to Poland, the train to Poland—the one that stops in the village of Oscheweim outside of Krakow, where the air has been gray for seventy years.

When I visited Krakow as an adult, I went next door to Kazimertz, its Jewish sister city next door. I walk the empty former market place to look at historical photos of that same square bustling and crowded. I spent the next day in a national art museum, afraid to do the day trip to Auschwitz. There is no escaping the memory of Holocaust in Poland. Every artist whose work hangs in the museum died in 1942. The year the Nazis gassed the artists and musicians. I walked through the museum having to turn the lights on and off in each room as I entered and left. I was all alone there. I stood in the museum with watery eyes. It was like a dream. I could not move.

The cemetery that became the stepfather's and my cemetery interred its last body in 1920. It was unusual. Walking through Germany one becomes accustomed to Catholic and Protestant cemeteries and stark scattered monuments to the Jews—but no Jewish cemeteries. And unlike any pristine German cemetery with scarcely a leaf out of place the day after a big wind, the cemetery of Werms was overgrown and messy.

The gate was black wrought iron and slanted—the foundation buckling on one side. The oak trees hung low to ground. I made chairs out of the low branches. The stepfather photographed me there on black and white film. The grasses were nearly knee high. It was more a meadow with a bit of stone than a cemetery.

The stones were cracked and on their sides. They had moss growing on them and were stained in bird shit. Some had fallen forward and obscured the inscriptions. Some had pushed back against the ground and looked like the very tablets of Moses. They were all in Hebrew. The unyielding script looking magical in its demise. Sit next to that one, the stepfather would say. It will be a good photo. I did what I was told, stood among the forgotten graves. The stepfather smirked and clicked. I posed without smile. He never asked me to. Never tried to get one.

I was dumb then. I asked him why. Why doesn't anyone come and keep up this graveyard? Why does it look like Halloween? Why does the writing look spooky? Why do I feel haunted and followed?

Those that would care for these graves are all dead, he said. Anyone who would have taken care of these ancestral graves is dead or gone to America and now, of course, old. It hits me in a strange deluge of tears. He asks me to stand in front of another tree, the branches gnarled and pointing to a grave that is heaved on its side. The date is 1903. I begin to clean it, pull back the weeds and debris so that the Hebrew name can be read clearly. I blow air across the surface and into the ravines of lettering and debris.

What are you now, the last Jew in Germany? You are ruining the photo. He mocks me. I don't answer him. I move away from it. He takes my photo. I move again and he takes another one. It's good, he says, that I'm crying—it works for the mood of the place. I look above the lens at his blonde balding head.

"There's no one to take care of the graves," I yell to him. "Doesn't that bother you?" But I'm whimpering now; I'm in that hyperventilation that happens when you try to speak, breathe and cry at the same time.

"I know," he says, "that's what makes it so cool to photograph. Looks spooky."

"But there's no one to take care of the graves," I say. How can I explain anything more to him? This is fucked up. You don't take your adolescent stepdaughter to abandoned Jewish cemeteries in Germany to film her crying. What's wrong with you? But I don't know how to say this yet.

He continues to film me crying. The pretty melancholy skirt he picked out for me this morning now feels more and more like a prop. I try to ignore him and cry in peace, my spirit sinks into my flesh. I feel heavy. I am twelve, American, and know nothing of history. But I find pebbles on the ground and place them on any headstone that is level enough for them to stay without rolling off. It seems as if that's where they are meant to be. I find out in Krakow years later that pebbles on tombstones are a form of prayer. But on that day I whispered to the stones that I am sorry to be here this way. That I'll try and clean up despite the stepfather yelling at me that I'm ruining the set by pulling weeds and placing pebbles. I pray to the tombstones for forgiveness. A holocaust, I realize, has occurred when there is no one left to attend the graves.

I fly there now when I have those dreams. Or part of me flies there. Just above the treetops till I get there. When I return I am finally alone. He is not there anymore. There is no camera. I sit on one of those low, low branches and watch the stillness. The ground has taken over some of the graves now. I try to decipher the Hebrew on the few tombstones still standing. I think I can make out beloved, mother, daughter, sister, father, son, brother. What else is there?

David Breeden

Nineteen Fifty Eight

The story goes that my father got laid off just days before I was born. In order to pay the hospital bill—and thereby retrieve me—my father had to borrow $250.00 from my mom's father, who had to sell one of his Black Angus beef cows to the slaughterhouse to raise the money.

So, I was born on hope and credit, which has remained the story of my life.

I was conceived in Orange, Texas near the shipyards where my father had a job welding on ships. (Janis Joplin lived there at the time, too, though we never met.) When my mother was seven months pregnant, my dad got laid off and so we were off to Granite City, Illinois, an industrial town on the Mississippi River. My father was a welder on a production line for Sherman tanks, but the line closed down, as I mentioned, days before I was born. The Korean War had been good for Sherman tanks. But that was over. When I was three weeks old—thanks to the sacrifice of the cow—we moved to Eastern Tennessee. But I don't remember living there either.

My father belonged to the Boilermakers Union and we traveled from job to job all over the Midwest and South. For housing, we owned a fifteen-foot trailer that we pulled from place to place. It was made of canvas, a leftover from temporary government housing during the Second World War. It was shaped like a loaf of bread, not like a cracker box. The trailers had started life as Army regulation olive green, but the people who bought them painted them all the colors of the rainbow and many that are not in the rainbow. Ours was lavender. My gut belief that nothing is solid perhaps stems from the fact that my childhood home was not only movable but could be shaken with one hand...

I woke up on the sandy soil of the piney woods of northern Louisiana. I remember the soil because in my first memory I am crawling, trying to catch a cat that had run under our mobile home. I think I was two years old. My mother had warned and warned me about the coral snakes. I had never seen one of those, but I was deathly afraid of the lizards that I knew dwelt under the trailer. But I was single-minded in my pursuit of the cat, whose life I had uncomprehendingly made miserable by such experiments as trying to drive a nail into it.

As I reached for the cat—who had cowered into the dim shadow—blinded as I was coming out of the searing Louisiana sun, I did not see that I was reaching for a fishhook. As I grasped for the cat, the fishhook sank into my flesh, to stay.

We had one car, and my dad was gone to work. My mother ran, holding me, madly searching for someone in the trailer park with a car. All I could think of was the horror of having someone open my aching fist to remove the fishhook. I suspect that I remember this so well because it is when I discovered I did not control the next hours of my life. Others would do what they thought best without consulting me. This was shocking news.

When the fishhook goes in, it has to come out.

Gloria Jean Harris

Who am I?

I wish I knew, sometimes I think I am this seventy-one year old hip grandmother of three children and six grands who have been there...and Lord have I been there and would never go back to anytime in my life.

I remember a very lonely childhood, four older siblings, a hard-working mother, and a lazy father. He did not like to work, was unable to keep any job for long, and was a drinking man. All that made my mother's job harder, and kept her upset all of the time. That did not leave a soft, warm and loving time for us children.

So, my older brother became my answer to and for everything. He reached down to me, and I reached up. Things were well for a while in my small and safe world.

Let me ask a question: can the sun shine too bright? I think so because it was that way on this day in May, 1948, when my safe world was shattered into a million pieces, never to be put back together again. The airplane came out of the sky to crash into my house, killed two of my brothers, altered my mother's heart and soul, reduced my father into even less of a husband and father.

So, for the next eleven years there are fading memories of a teenage life. It came and went without fanfare, just more pain. At eighteen, I became a mother, and then a wife; yes, in that order. He was a good man, but was not able to detach himself from his mother in order to shape his own life. There goes my young adult life. It was filled with too much hard work. Too many headaches, non-existing help. Talking about being alone? Divorced at the young age of thirty-one.

I failed to mention that during those eleven years I lost my two remaining brothers—remember my lifeline? He was lost to me at the age of fifteen in a car crash (again it was a bright shining day). Seven years later another bright sun shining day in January (the first Super Bowl Sunday) my dear brother (who'd reached down to me) was called to heaven.

Ok, enough is enough! Time to change my life, so I thought. However, God's idea of change was very different from mine, because at the age of thirty-six, breast cancer reared its ugly head. The sun was really shining that day that I drove myself to the doctor's office to find out this bad news alone.

Thirty years later, moving along dealing with several medical problems, I still don't see the dark clouds, or hear the thunder, see the lighting flashing. I only see the bright sunshine and look forward to each day that I can look up, give thanks, and move on.

Who am I?

I know I am a daughter, a sister, a mother, a grandmother, and a friend.

I am Gloria.

CoCo Harris

I am

And who am I?
I am
her daughter.
I am
CoCo.

CONTRIBUTORS

DEBRA BAKER graduated with a degree in English Literature, was a health care provider for twnty-five years, and is an award-winning documentary filmmaker. Her films aired on PBS and screened at film festivals across the U.S. and the U.K. She wrote, produced, directed, and edited *Broken Ties*, her award-winning debut video—which is a personal documentary about being an unwed mother in 1967, having to give the baby up for adoption, and living with the life-long effects on birthmothers. Her second video, *Lost and Found*, is Ms. Baker's documentary about searching for, and finding, the son she relinquished for adoption thirty years before. She is a frequent presenter at adoption conferences in the U.S. and Canada, where she screens her films and leads workshops. Her writing has appeared widely in adoption publications, and she was awarded the Excellence in Broadcast Media Award by the American Adoption Congress. She was published in *5x5 Literary Magazine*, and lives in Northern California where she continues to work on her memoir.

RICHARD BALLON is a member of the Dramatist's Guild and his work has been performed in NYC at Sola Voces/Estrogenius Festival, Stage Left's: Women at Work, MamaDrama and Left Out Festival, Emerging Artist Theater's: One Man Talking, and NativeAlien's Short Stories 5; also at The Universal Theater in Provincetown, Out of the Blue Gallery in Cambridge, Shea Theater in Turners Falls, Devanaughan Theater in Boston, Dylan Thomas Festival in Chicago, Walking the Wire in Iowa City, Insipirato Festival in Toronto, Asphalt Shorts In Kitchener and ArtHotel in Montreal.

DIANE HOOVER BECHTLER lives in Charlotte, North Carolina, with her husband, Michael Gross, who is a poet with a day job, and with their cat.

MADELEINE BECKMAN is the author of *Dead Boyfriends*, a poetry collection (Linear Arts Books). She is the recipient of awards and grants including a New York Foundation for the Arts Award for fiction and a Poetry Society of America award for poetry, and Irish Arts Council Award Fundaçion Valparaiso grant. Her poetry, fiction, and memoir has appeared nationally and internationally in journals and anthologies including the *Southern Poetry Review, Barrow Street, Confrontation*, and *Tempus: A Journal of Literature and the Arts*. Madeleine teaches at the City University of New York, and is a contributing editor and writer for *The Literary Journal* (Fairleigh Dickinson University) and *Bellevue Literary Journal*.

J.D. BLAIR is a writer of short fiction, poetry, and scripts for the stage whose work has appeared in several literary magazines including, *Pearl, Writer's Journal, Carve Magazine, Third Wednesday* and *Fog City Review*.

MARTHA EVERHART BRANIFF's novel, *Step Over Rio*, is forthcoming (The Way Things Are Publications), and won the Writer's League of Texas Mystery/Adventure Novel Award. Her book of short fiction and poems, *Songs from the Bone Closet* (Stone River Press) was a finalist in the Writer's League of Texas Violet Crown Award for Literary Fiction and Poetry. She has been nominated for the Pushcart Prize for her short story "Resurrection;" and for an essay about children of the Holocaust, "Voices Calling." *Beds of Broken Glass,* her first novel, was a finalist for the Bellwether Prize. *Sold*, a screenplay, won the Santa Fe Actor's Choice Award. She has been a juried poet at the Houston Poetry Fest and her work also includes the chapbook *The Fringe: A Nurse's Notes* (A Writer's Choice); and her fiction, essays and poetry have been published in numerous journals and anthologies. Her work with abused children and child immigrants began in the late seventies. She founded Child Advocates, Inc., and she has won numerous community awards including Inc. Magazine's Entrepreneur of the Year, Houston Mayor's Award, Volunteer of the Year; Houston Bar Association Liberty Bell Award; and YWCA Woman of the Year.

REGINA MURRAY BRAULT has twice been nominated for the Pushcart Prize. Her awards include the 2007 Euphoria and Sysaje Enterprises Poetry Competitions, and the 2008 Creekwalker Prize. Her poetry has appeared in more than 130 different publications.

DOUGLAS G. CAMPBELL is a professor of art at George Fox University. His poems have appeared in *Borderlands, Windhover, Into the Teeth of the Wind, RiverSedge* and many other publications. His artworks have been included in over 170 juried and invitational exhibits across the country.

YU-HAN CHAO was born and grew up in Taipei, Taiwan, and received her MFA from Penn State. The Backwaters Press published her poetry collection, *We Grow Old*, in 2008. For more writing and artwork, visit www.yuhanchao.com.

CASEY CLABOUGH is the author of the travel memoir *The Warrior's Path: Reflections Along an Ancient Route* as well as four scholarly books about contemporary writers. He serves as editor of the literature section of *Encyclopedia Virginia* and as general editor of the *James Dickey Review*. His first novel, *Confederado*, will appear in 2012, as will his fifth scholarly book, *Inhabiting Contemporary Southern & Appalachian Literature: Region & Place in the 21st Century*.

BETH LYNN CLEGG lives in Houston, Texas. This octogenarian has been published in a variety of genres since beginning her writing career after retiring from other endeavors. An animal lover with two cats, she also enjoys gardening, reading and church activities. She treasures two children, four grandchildren, and myriad friends.

ELAYNE CLIFT is an award-winning writer whose work has appeared internationally; and most recently in *Poets & Writers Magazine, The Chronicle of Higher Education*, and *Vermont Magazine*. She lives in Saxtons River, VT.

After thirty years as a behavioral science researcher and author ALAN COHEN discovered poetry and truffles in Tuscany. So he retired and now devotes his time to pursuing both passions.

KAREN de BALBIAN VERSTER, four-time breast and ovarian cancer survivor, is the author of the novel, *Boob, A Story of Sex, Cancer & Stupidity*. Many of her stories, essays and poems have been published in literary reviews and anthologies, most recently "Rapists I Have Known and Loved," accepted for the 2011 anthology, *Book of Villains*, Main Street Rag Pub., "Anne Frank Redux" in the 2010 anthology, *Writers and Their Notebooks*, University of South Carolina Press, which prompted a The Writer reviewer to describe Karen de Balbian Verster as a writer who "recalled [her] inaugural journal with clarity…", "Her Eighth Gray Hair" in the 2010 anthology, *When Last on the Mountain: Essays, Stories, and Poems from Writers over 50*, (Holy Cow! Press), which a Star Tribune review described as "Karen de Balbian Verster's exuberant celebration of middle age," and "The Bad Seed" which won Honorable Mention in the UNO Writing Contest. To read excerpts and more about the author visit: http://mysite.verizon.net/kdebv.

SUMMER DeNAPLES graduated from St. Olaf College with a Bachelor of Arts in English and Political Science. She is a member of the Free Association poetry club, and an aspiring writer.

REBECCA T. DICKINSON works as a substitute teacher, freelance writer and editor. The Law Related Education division of the South Carolina Bar published a lesson plan packet entitled Equal Justice, which Dickinson co-wrote and co-designed. Creative work from her tentative story collection, *Red*

Loam, has been published by *The Copperfield Review* (Autumn 2011), and by *Dew on the Kudzu* (September 2011). The story collection is connected to her book manuscript, *Sons of the Edisto*. Both works feature R.T. Dickinson as her byline. Dickinson raises her one-year-old son, Charles, in South Carolina.

CHRISTINE DONOVAN journals daily for insight and pleasure, and tries to live by the motto "to thine own self be true." She is an artist and poet. The central coast of California is her home. Best of all, she got out alive!

GINA FERRARA received her MFA from the University of New Orleans and works as an educator. In 2006, her chapbook, *The Size of Sparrows*, was published by Finishing Line Press. Her poems have appeared in numerous journals including: *The Poetry Ireland Review, The Briar Cliff Review*, and *Callaloo*. Trembling Pillow Press published her collection *Ethereal Avalanche* in 2009. She has poems forthcoming in *The New Laurel Review*.

CARMEN ANTHONY FIORE is a former social worker and schoolteacher and is presently a full-time writer/editor. He has published books (adult/juvenile/young adult literature, fiction and nonfiction) as well as short stories, articles and essays (print and online) for adults. He has sold five options to his feature film screenplays to independent movie producers in southern California. He is a Rider University (Lawrenceville, NJ) alumnus, and a Rutgers University Graduate School of Education (New Brunswick, NJ) alumnus. He presently has twelve digital books (fiction/nonfiction, adult/juvenile) available from Amazon.com Kindle e-book reader store, with more on the way in the near future.

SARA GLENN FORTSON is a native of Georgia. She obtained an undergraduate degree in Journalism and a M.Ed. from the University of Georgia. She currently lives happily in the Chicago area where she has found a wonderfully supportive and active writing community. Sarah Glenn has two beautiful daughters and a best friend named Rick.

MARGARET ELYSIA GARCIA lives in the far northern corner of California. She is working on a memoir of growing up on a military base in West Germany in the 1980s.

LEWIS GARDNER is a writer and actor who lives in the Catskill Mountains of New York State. His prose, poems, and plays have been published throughout the English-speaking world, including *Best American Short Plays*

2008-2009 and Macmillan of Australia's Comedy. "Memory" is one of a series of memoirs of his New England origins. He can be seen in the current season of "Celebrity Ghost Stories" haunting Mia Tyler.

SHELLY CLARK GEISER is a poet, an educator and speaker. She is the author of *The Cockroach Monologues, Vol. 1*, (Zero Street Books, 2011), a chapbook of insect persona poems. Shelly presented poetry programs at the national conference of the Entomological Society of America in November of 2011. She co-edited an anthology of interviews and works by Nebraska writers: *Road Trip: Conversations With Writers*, (Backwaters Press, 2003). The book was selected for two Nebraska Book Awards, Best Anthology and Best Design. Shelly's poetry has been anthologized in *Times of Sorrow, Times of Grace* and *Nebraska Presence: An Anthology of Poetry*. She has poems in the forthcoming anthologies *The Memories Project* (Ridges Sanctuary, Wisconsin), and *An Untidy Season* (Backwaters Press). Shelly earned a B.A. from the University of Nebraska, Kearney and a Masters Degree at the University of Nebraska, Lincoln. She lives in Omaha.

DENI ANN GEREIGHTY is a native of New Orleans, and spent twenty years in the Pacific Northwest as a traveling nurse, mostly in Labor & Delivery. She has published poetry, health care articles, a chapter in *The Lesbian Health Book*, journal entries and prose. Deni Ann is owned by two feline companions, and is delighted to have three young nieces to help raise.

MAC GREENE has a PhD in Clinical Psychology and runs a general practice with specializations in adolescence, couples, gay and transgender issues. He has been writing for five years, with publications in *Ars Medica, Marco Polo, bottle rockets, Tipton Poetry Journal, Hawai'i Pacific Review*, and *Poetry of Yoga*. He has a fondness for Haiku and Haibun, and hopes to continue "emerging" as a writer.

SUSAN GRIER's work most recently appeared in *Dear John, I Love Jane: Women Write About Leaving Men for Women*. She is writing a memoir about growing up southern, raising a transgender child, and discovering her inner lesbian at age fifty-one.

GLORIA JEAN HARRIS is a seventy-two year old hip grandmother of six and mother of three who is also a daughter, sister, and a friend.

DaMARIS B. HILL is a doctoral candidate in the English-Creative Writing Program at the University of Kansas. She won the 2003 Hurston/Wright

Award for Short Fiction. Hill's work appears in: *Blue Island Review, Shadowbox, Tongues of the Ocean, Kweli Journal, Sleet Magazine, Reverie, Bermuda Anthology of Poetry, Warpland, Mourning Katrina: A Poetic Response to Tragedy*, and *Women in Judaism*.

BRADLEY EARLE HOGE has published three chapbooks, and his poetry appears in numerous journals and anthologies worldwide including *Chronogram, Rattle, Tertulia, Stickman Review, Tonapah la, entelechy: mind and culture*, and *Tar Wolf Review*.

EXSULO ILLUSTRO is a globe trekker and extreme realist. Exsulo ponders the human existence through the lens of psychobiological-socioeconomic paradigms. He is the introvert's extrovert who relishes his space to explore and observe our essentialism.

RAUD KENNEDY is a writer and dog trainer in Portland, Oregon. To learn about his most recent work, *Portland*, a collection of short stories, please visit www.raudkennedy.com.

JACQUELINE KOLOSOV has published three young adult novels including *A Sweet Disorder* (2009) and *The Red Queen's Daughter* (2007), both from Hyperion. She was awarded an NEA Literature Fellowship in Prose and also won the Mozelle Memoir Competition for "Souvenir."

KRISTIN LAUREL is a mother of three, a nurse, and growing up to be a poet. She is completing her first book of poetry entitled *Giving Them All Away*. Some recent publications include work in *Calyx, Evening Street Review, Grey Sparrow, Main Street Rag, The Mom Egg, Naugatuck Review, Prose Poem Project* and other journals. She is a recent graduate of a Poetry apprenticeship at The Loft Literary Center (Minneapolis). She has a chapbook forthcoming, *You Might Feel A Little Poke* (Pudding House Press 2012).

CATHERINE LEE is from Virginia Beach, Virginia where she grew up minutes away from the Atlantic Ocean. Seven years ago, she relocated to Texas where she currently lives with her husband and two kids. Her poetry has appeared in the *Blinn Literary Journal, Wilderness House Literary Review*, and *Prompted*.

JANINE LEHANE is from Brisbane, Australia and is a graduate of The College of William and Mary in Williamsburg, Virginia. While at William and Mary, she was the coordinator of a state-wide program for promising student authors. Now Janine teaches in an M.Ed. program at Columbia College in South Carolina and lives in the Blue Ridge Mountains of Western North Carolina.

BARBARA LEWIS is a longtime copyeditor whose work has appeared in San Francisco magazine, the San Francisco Chronicle, PC World, and a number of other publications. She lives in San Francisco with her husband, Bob, and their giant dachshund, Shorty.

RUSS ALLISON LOAR has written poetry and short fiction for decades but only published during the last few years. The demanding hours of being a newspaper reporter left little time for anything but the writing itself. His last years in journalism were spent writing for the Los Angeles Times, followed by teaching news writing at Orange Coast College in Orange County, California, and graduate studies in American literature. Before a life in journalism, Russ was a musician and songwriter. He continues to write and record music sporadically, see http://russloarmusic.com. Russ also dabbles in photography and his photos are occasionally used by various web sites, such as the Nature Conservancy. He has a steady trickle of readers from around the world at his poetry site: http://writingapoem.com.

NANCY LUBARSKY writes from New Jersey. She has been an educator for twenty-five years and is currently a superintendent. She has been published in *Edison Literary Review* and *Exit 13 Magazine*. One of her poems was recently nominated for a Pushcart Prize.

MONICA S. MACANSANTOS earned her bachelors degree in Creative Writing, magna cum laude, from the University of the Philippines in 2007. Her fiction, poetry, and non-fiction have appeared in the *Philippines Free Press, Phati'tude Literary Magazine, Quarterly Literary Review Singapore, Sunday Inquirer Magazine, Philippine Daily Inquirer, Philippine Panorama, Home Life*, and *The Evening Paper*. She taught literature and writing at the University of the Philippines for three years. She is currently completing her MFA in Fiction at the Michener Center for Writers.

DEBORAH L. J. MACKINNON's South Dakota farm heritage flavors her writing, as does the fact that she's raised three children and taught secondary school for over twenty years. She enjoys encouraging writing in her students and in the general public. She's proud of residing on the Puget Sound in Washington where she and other poets were featured in a public arts project in 2005. She co-authored professional research funded by Pi Lambda Theta in 2004, and a literary publication included her short story "End Rows" in 2001. She has maintained "Imitations of Keats" at http://drmackinnon.wordpress.com for the past several years. She currently teaches creative writing as well as advises for the debate team at Kingston High School, Kingston, Washington.

TERRY MARTIN has published over 250 poems, articles, and essays, and has edited journals, books, and anthologies. Her second book of poems, *The Secret Language of Women*, was published by Blue Begonia Press in 2006.

JASMINNE MENDEZ is a performance poet, actress, teacher and published writer. Over the last nine years she has performed her poetry in venues all around Houston. She has worked extensively as a teaching artist with the Alley Theatre, KIPP Houston charter schools and currently at Cristo Rey Jesuit. Her publishing credits include her memoir piece "The China Cabinet" in the anthology *Windows Into My World: Latino Youth Write their Lives*, edited by Sarah Cortez (Arte Publico Press); and a nano fiction piece "Grandeur" published by Flash: The International Short-Story Magazine out of England.

W. K. MEDLEN was born and raised in the Rocket City, Huntsville Alabama. He attended the University of Alabama in Tuscaloosa and earned a Bachelor's in English and minored in Creative Writing. He is currently wrapping up his Masters in English at The University of Alabama in Huntsville. W. K. Medlen loves his wife, Meghan Brown Medlen, enjoys cycling and playing music, prefers late nights to early mornings, considers himself an amateur beer connoisseur, and believes in Truth, Faith, Hope, and Love.

MARIANGELA MIHAI is a poet and visual artist, and is originally from Romania. She is studying Anthropology at Emory University and is the president of the university's Ethics and the Arts Society. She believes that being a decent human being is not only necessary to being a good artist, but also more important. To see more of her work, visit www.romanianpoet.com.

LINDA MUSSILLO is a special education teacher and Program Coordinator of the Adults with Disabilities Program at Santa Fe College in Gainesville, Florida. Her totally blind father and legally blind mother provided the author with an unusual childhood rich with memories and revelations, many of which find their way into her writing.

DAVE MORRISON is a poet whose current work includes *Clubland*, a collection of poems about rock bars written in verse (Fighting Cock Press, 2011). After years of playing guitar in rock & roll bars in Boston and NYC he currently resides in coastal Maine.

CARI OLESKEWICZ is a writer living in Tampa. Her work has appeared in *The Washington Post, Italian Cooking and Living, New York Magazine, Sassee Magazine*, and *Epiphany Magazine*. She has recently completed writing a novel-in-verse.

ALBA POKU (Dr. MONIQUE LESLIE AKASSI) is an author, professor, radio host, and humanitarian. She is currently an Assistant Professor of English Composition and Rhetoric at Virginia Union University and holds a Ph.D. in English Composition and Rhetoric with minors in Literary Criticism Theory and African American Literature. Her works have been published both nationally and internationally. She is the author of *Neo Hybrid Pedagogy in Post Colonialism Composition: An Investigation On Writing Portfolios For African American Students;* and *Postcolonial Composition Pedagogy: Using The Culture of Marginalized Students To Teach Writing*. Her work has been published in the *Encyclopedia of African American Popular Culture*, the *CEA Mag*, and *The Zora Neale Hurston Forum.* Her scholarship includes composition pedagogy, rhetorical criticism, issues in American education, and her recently coined theory, "post-colonial composition pedagogies and praxis." Read more at www.monique-akassi.com.

MAMIE POTTER is a writing student of Angela Davis-Gardner and Peggy Payne. She lives in Raleigh, North Carolina. "The Golf Course Grass" was the winner in a short story contest judged by Elizabeth Berg.

CHERRI RANDALL is currently Assistant Professor of English at the University of Pittsburgh, Johnstown. She has a PhD in English Literature and an MFA in Creative Writing from the University of Arkansas. Her work has appeared in *Mid-America Poetry Review, Lake Effect, So to Speak, Paper Street Press, Permafrost Review, Paddlefish, The Potomac Review, storySouth, Blue Earth Review*, and *Sojourn*. She has green eyes, fiery red hair, and arms spattered with freckles. She lives with two teenaged daughters, a Chihuahua named Zora for Zora Neale Hurston, and high hopes for the future.

ROBERT REID-PHARR is a writer and teacher who lives and works in New York City. A native North Carolinian, he holds a B.A. in Political Science from the University of North Carolina at Chapel Hill as well as a Ph.D. from

Yale. Reid-Pharr is a Distinguished Professor at the CUNY Graduate Center. He has published three books, including one of the most acclaimed treatments of nineteenth century black writing, *Conjugal Union: The Body, the House, and the Black American* (Oxford University Press, 1999), an award winning collection of essays, *Black Gay Man* (NYU Press, 2001), and most recently a study of mid-twentieth century African American literature and culture, *Once You Go Black: Choice, Desire, and the Black Intellectual* (NYU Press, 2007).

CAROL J. RHODES' work, including short stories, essays, poetry, non-fiction, and plays has appeared in such publications and newspapers as *Houston Chronicle, Christian Science Monitor, Stroud (England) News & Journal, The Houston Press*; magazines *Country Home, Good Old Boat*, and *Texas*; as well as numerous journals and anthologies. She has won several literary awards for both poetry and prose. One of her plays, *Comin' Home to Burnstown*, was showcased in a summer play festival in an off-Broadway theater. In addition to creative writing, Carol presents business writing seminars for university and corporate clients.

ZACK ROGOW is the author, editor, or translator of nineteen books or plays. His seventh book of poems, *My Mother and the Ceiling Dancers*, will be published by Kattywompus Press in 2012. His poems have appeared in a variety of magazines, from American Poetry Review to Zyzzyva. He is the editor of an anthology of U.S. poetry, *The Face of Poetry*, published by the University of California Press in 2005. Currently he teaches in the MFA in Writing Program at the California College of the Arts and in the low-residency MFA at the University of Alaska, Anchorage.

HELEN RUGGIERI has found the perfect form for memoirs - the Japanese haibun which is part prose and usually contains a haiku. Read more about Helen's work by visiting www.HelenRuggieri.com.

NAN RUSH is a poet and musician who has been published in *Rolling Stone, Poets On, Yet Another Small Magazine, Thirteen*, and *Rambunctious Review*. She has completed the first draft of a fantasy novel, and is working on a memoir.

RIKKI SANTER's work has appeared in various publications including *Ms. Magazine, Poetry East, Margie, Asphodel, Alabama Literary Review, Potomac Review, The Adirondack Review, Grimm*, and *The Main Street Rag*. Rikki's poetry collection, *Front Nine: A Biography of Place* was published by Kulipi

Press. Her second collection, *Clothesline Logic,* was published by Pudding House as finalist in their national chapbook competition.

JUDITH SERIN's collection of poetry, *Hiding in the World,* was published by Diane di Prima's Eidolon Editions, and her *Davs Without (Sky): A Poem Tarot,* seventy-eight short prose poems in the form of a tarot deck with illustration and book art design by Nikki Thompson, is forthcoming from Deconstructed Artichoke Press. She writes fiction as well as poetry, and her work has appeared in numerous magazines and anthologies, including *Bachy, The Ohio Journal, Writer's Forum, Nebraska Review, Woman's World, Colorado State Review,* and *Barnabe Mountain Review.* Most recently she has published prose poems/memoirs in the anthologies *Proposing on the Brooklyn Bridge* (Grayson Books) and *When Last on the Mountain,* (Holy Cow! Press); in the journals *The Paterson Literary Review, First Intensity, Paragraph,* and *the blink;* and in a chapbook of nine prose poems, *Family Stories* (Deconstructed Artichoke Press). She teaches literature and creative writing at California College of the Arts and lives in San Francisco with her husband, Herbert Yee.

W. CLAYTON SCOTT is Poet Laureate of Fayetteville, Arkansas, and is the author and performer of the one-person play, *Down in Littletown.* He holds a Masters of Fine Arts in Writing in Poetry from Spalding University and is the author of volumes of poetry, including *Mind Your Head,* and *Sex, and Other Matters of Regard.* He has ranked in the top ten percent of slam poets in the world and represented Arkansas in the National Poetry Slams. He has won numerous awards for his poetry. He was chosen as a poetry ambassador with the Arkansas Arts in Education program and is the founder of Student Poetry Movement. Clayton worked as a comedian for more than twenty years; and he taught school in Oklahoma before becoming a television producer for a local and nationally syndicated TV talk show. Clayton serves as a part of three Arkansas Arts Council programs. He is an avid photographer with an eye for unusual and common images. Learn more about his poetry, plays and photography at www.ClaytonScott.com

NOELLE SICKELS is author of the historical novels *Walking West, The Shopkeeper's Wife,* and *The Medium,* and has just completed *Out of Love,* about a birthmother tracking the mysterious disappearance of her grown son. Sickles' story "In Domestic Service" won the annual fiction award from the literary journal *Zone 3.*

RICK SMITH is a clinical psychologist specializing in brain damage and domestic violence. He plays the harmonica and writes for the Los Angeles-based group The Mescal Sheiks, and has published widely. His most recent book is *Hard Landing* (Lummox Press) is about the legacy and mythology of the wren.

ALEX STEIN's work has appeared recently in, or is forthcoming from, *The Agni Review* (online), *The Bellingham Review, The Gulf Coast Review, Harper's Magazine* (online), *Hotel Amerika, Kearney Street Books, Nazraeli Press, The Pinch,* and *The Literary Review.* His books include the genre bending memoir, *Made-Up Interviews with Imaginary Artists* (Ugly Duckling Presse, 2009) and *Weird Emptiness* (Wings Press, 2007). He received his Ph.D. in Creative Writing from the University of Denver in 2007 and currently lives in Boulder, Colorado.

NANCY SKALLA is a native of the Midwest, who grabbed life's excitement by trying new things. From teaching to real estate, Red Cross to prose, she marvels every day at what a great time in history this is to be alive.

PAUL SOHAR ended his higher education with a BA in philosophy and took a day job in a research lab while writing in every genre, publishing seven volumes of translations. Now a volume of his own poetry *Homing Poems* is available from Iniquity Press. His latest is *The Wayward Orchard*, published by Wordrunner e-Chapbooks in 2011. He contributed the lyrics to a musical *G-d is Something Gorgeous* that premiered in Scranton, PA in 2007. His magazine credits include *Agni, Kenyon Review, Rattle, Seneca Review,* and more.

DOROTHY STONE was raised in the Midwest and transplanted to the East coast. To pursue a dream of appearing on Broadway, she moved to New York, married, became a mother, and then a teacher to help support the family. She is now retired and happily having time to spend on her writing.

BARB TARTRO is a retired surgical heart ICU RN and Indiana University adjunct faculty member. Ms. Tatro is the mother of four and grandmother of seven. She spends her unassigned hours writing, playing piano, painting, sketching, sculpting, and photographing the idiosyncrasies of this world. She is currently in the process of publishing her first book, *To Death We Owe the Truth*, an expose' of her years in healthcare.

ELEANOR VINCENT is the author of the memoir *Swimming with Maya* (Capital Books, 2004). She lives and writes in Oakland, California. Visit her at www.eleanorvincent.com.

TAMARA W. publishes here under a pseudonym. Her work has appeared in the *San Francisco Bay Guardian, 5 Finger Review, Outside, Alaska, Salt* and on America Public Media/Weekend America. In addition to a wide-range of exotic and painstaking day jobs, Tamara has worked as a cliché-whoring reporter for various daily and weekly publications, which her work has been included in.

AHREND R. TORREY is a Mississippi poet and painter. His poetry relates to nature and God, but most of all life, and what he experiences through his life journey. He attended Mississippi Gulf Coast Honors College and is currently working toward a graduate degree in English at William Carey University. He received the MGCCC Creative Writing Award in 2010, and won first place in categories of haiku and prose poetry at the 2011 Creative Writing Competition. Ahrend lives in a 12x24 building he has dubbed "The Poet Shack," and makes his home in rural, Mississippi.

GREGG WEATHERBY has two previous books of poetry: *Under Orion* (Pudding House Publications) and *Bone Island* (Finishing Line Press). He lives in upstate NY and is a lecturer at SUNY Cortland.

SARAH BROWN WEITZMAN has had well over 200 poems published in numerous journals. Her second chapbook, *The Forbidden* (Pudding House 2003) was followed by *Never Far from Flesh*, a full-length volume of poems (Pure Heart/Main Street Rag, 2005).

AMBER L. WEST is a writer, attorney, and social worker who lives and works in San Francisco. She is currently working on her first novel. Recently, one of her neighbors left on her doorstep two and a half homemade cupcakes, with two and a half candles, in celebration of Amber reaching two and a half years cancer-free.

BETH WINEGARNER is a poet, author and journalist whose poems have appeared in New Verse News, Terrain, Tertulia, Bardsong and Lime Green Bulldozers and *What's Nature Got to Do with Me? Staying Wildly Sane in a Mad World* from Native West Press. Her books include *Sacred Sonoma, Read the Music*, and *Beloved*. She blogs on teen influences and moral panics at Backward Messages (http://backwardmessages.wordpress.com). She lives in San Francisco with her partner and daughter. For more, visit http://www.bethwinegarner.com.

KIRBY WRIGHT was a Visiting Fellow at the 2009 International Writers Conference in Hong Kong, where he represented the Pacific Rim region of Hawaii. He was also a Visiting Writer at the 2010 Martha's Vineyard Residency in Edgartown, Mass., and the 2011 Artist in Residence at Milkwood International, Czech Republic. He is the author of the companion novels *Punahou Blues* and *Moloka'i Nui Ahina*, both set in the islands.

NICOLE R. ZIMMERMAN's work appears in the Los Angeles Times and in *The Best Women's Travel Writing 2009*. She attends the MFA in Writing program at the University of San Francisco and blogs at http://paper-pencil-pen.blogspot.com.

ABOUT THE EDITOR

CoCo Harris lives for story.

Her story began in Atlanta, GA, and has traversed the Nation's capital, West Africa, Seattle, WA, Louisville, KY, Coastal Georgia, and the Susquehanna Valley. Though she now lives in central PA, CoCo is particularly at home anywhere sun and surf meet.

She earned a B.S. in Electrical Engineering at Howard University, did graduate work in African Studies, and began her Intellectual Property Law career working for the Patent and Trademark Office while becoming a wife and a mother of three daughters. She later entered the US Patent Bar becoming a patent law professional representing individuals, firms, and corporations in the US and abroad.

CoCo received her Master of Fine Arts in Writing in Fiction from Spalding University, and is a Zora Neale Huston/Richard Wright Foundation alumna. As a lifetime diarist, she is drawn to personal narratives. For years she has guided others with crafting personal narratives through creative writing workshops and various memoir projects.

CoCo Harris is constantly exploring the notion of how we tell the stories of our lives.